PROCESS PERSON PRESENCE

•

A THEOLOGY FOR TODAY'S BELIEVERS

BY RAYMOND A. PARR

THE THOMAS MORE PRESS
Chicago, Illinois

ISBN 0-88347-263-5

TABLE OF CONTENTS

FOREWORD   5

1. INTRODUCTION TO THEOLOGY   10

2. PROCESS   16
    How It All Comes to Be
3. BIBLE   37
    Literature of the People of God
4. LIBERATION THEOLOGY   45
    Theology and Fundamentalism
5. BELIEVING IN CONTEXT   55
    More Than Doctrine and Dogma
6. SYMBOL AND MYTH   73
    Language of Faith
7. FAITH AND CULTURE   85
    Portrait of a Believer
8. SCRIPTURAL CONTEXT   107
    Real People and a Real World
9. RESURRECTION   120
    The Glory of Being Human
10. CHURCH   143
    All That is Going on with God
11. SPIRIT   162
    God Alive and Well in Us
12. SACRAMENT   168
    The Church at Work
13. MORALITY   195
    The Responsibility of Being Human
14. ANGELS   213
    Nothing Better Than Being Human
15. CHRISTOLOGY   221
    "Who Do You Say That I Am?"
16. THE QUESTION OF GOD   234
    An Answer Before the Question

FOREWORD

THEOLOGY IS NOT AUTHENTICATED by conformity to the past but by relevance to the present. An authentic theology arises from the faith experience of believing people in response to the real world of their ongoing faith experience. Our traditional theology was in its origin the response of the faith community upon entering a new world and a new age. An underground church that had been despised and persecuted became socially and culturally acceptable. A theology emerged that affirmed and proclaimed the cosmic dimension of that church and the reign of the Spirit, even in the universal and absolute categories of the culture of that world.

Today there is a new Pentecost in an expanding new world. In fact, there are three worlds, all new, in an expanding cosmos. In each of these worlds there is a church emerging from the catacombs into which it had retreated for safety and survival under threats, real or imagined. In our first world, the catacombs are institutions and structures of the culture itself into which the church has sought to defend itself against reformers, rationalists and modernists. In her defense, the church has claimed that her own static canonical structures, copied from the culture, are really of divine institution and enjoy a status of privilege and immunity from assessment or responsibility to justify their existence or performance. The new Pentecost is a new vision of authority, responsibility and expectation of credible performance from those who accept pastoral or ecclesiastical office.

In the second world, the catacombs are persons in labor camps and silence demanded by deterministic economic, social and political systems which are imposed as a way of life that exclude the freedom of the Gospel Way. In spite of threats and persecution, the good news is proclaimed and celebrated even where it is forbidden by the powers of the world.

In the third world, power, greed and cruelty sanctioned and supported by cultural, social and political institutions force the church to work silently behind closed doors where people of faith and spirit gather to hear the word of God and to share the Eucharist and the gift of the Spirit.

Every theology has come out of the darkness of catacombs to enlighten the faith of its own times. The function of a theology is to minister to the faith of the people.

Faith is the vision of the presence of God and the hearing of the Word when and where it is spoken. Theology ministers to believers by identifying the Word in the cultural, historical and total human context in which it is spoken. Theology presents the Word to the hearer and the hearer to the Word. Our world is new. A new world needs a new theology. Theology for our new world must be aware that change is a constant and that process is the substratum of all being and reality. Massive changes have taken place. The modern mind has gained marvelous insights into the mystery of the universe and into the mystery of human being and being human. We have more to believe, more to believe in, and more reason to believe than ever before. Revelation grows with the universe and with our understanding of it. Karl Marx, for example, made valid observations and predictions about the dynamic of human society and societal processes. History has shown his observations and predictions to be right; his "theology" was wrong. What he saw as "inexorable law" and "determinism," we must affirm as the movement of the spirit and freedom.

Charles Darwin's evolutionary view of the cosmic-life process does not threaten or reduce God's initiative in the creative process or threaten or reduce human dignity, but rather enhances both. God does not remove himself as creator by sharing his creative powers with his universe, but rather involves us more intimately with his own life and gives our life a cosmic dimension. We make the world God's kingdom by making it ours. The universe is the original "do it yourself" program; God's work is ultimately authenticated by our signature.

Sigmund Freud observed that the human personality was more than a composite of matter and spirit with philosophically and categorically defined potentialities and actualities. He discovered that the mystery of human personality could be penetrated and could be a valid subject for clinical observation and study. He saw that the mystery of human behavior was penetrable. What he saw as an observable and measurable phenomenon, we must proclaim and affirm as the human spirit in the image of God revealing to us by our own experience the glory of God and the dignity and value of being human.

Massive change in our world view has also been brought about by Albert Einstein. By rejecting the limits of the old absolutes, he has opened our minds to the mysteries of the universe and has opened the universe to the mystery of our minds. Einstein and our ancestor in faith, Abraham, in the Ancient Fertile Crescent were fascinated with the same mystery—the universe. Abraham's response was that this great universe needed and has a great constant God to keep it constant. Einstein saw such wonder, magnitude and energy in the universe that the god of the ancient theological categories was not adequate for his universe. A measured god cannot account for an immeasurable universe. This is our problem. We must see that we have imposed the measure of our cultural categories upon God and have insisted that God be in the image we have cast. Abraham must make friends with Einstein without compromise to the faith of Abraham or to the science of Einstein. Abraham must accept Einstein's vision of the universe and bring Einstein to his vision of God.

The task of theology and religious education is to be prophetic—to speak for God—to speak to our culture from our culture. Theology is authenticated by relevance to the present.

In the third world, the experience of institutional, social and economic oppression and the vision of hope of liberation have given rise to liberation theology. It is not a theology that validates the hope of liberation, but the hope of liberation that validates a theology.

In our world, we have been given new visions of the grandeur of the universe, of human dignity and freedom and the joy of being human. We are not threatened by the vision, but by the faithless fear that the vision is too good to be true. Our theology and religious education must come from faith in this vision which will validate our theology and religious education.

God is a transcending and benign creative presence whose name is a first person present tense affirmation, "I am here for you." First and second person pronouns transcend gender. "I and you" affirm an inclusive personal presence and identity on a level of awareness of interpresence which is our faith presence with God. Prayer is a "you and I" process and presence. We speak to God and God speaks to us. When we speak about God, God becomes a third person and our third person pronouns are categorically masculine, feminine and neuter, none of which is proper or adequate for speaking about God. Our need is not a personal pronoun that is genderless, but a personal pronoun that transcends gender without exclusion. Our neuter "it" certainly doesn't work because it denies the personal nature of God. "He" and she" are mutually exclusive and "it" is a denial of personal identity. Still, the pronoun is not really that important because our God wants to be named, known and called upon as the God of those who believe in him.

We are made and we speak in the image of God and we must maintain that order in our speaking to and about God. We must keep ourselves in the image of God and not begin to cast God in the image of ourselves. When we assign sexuality to

God, we are casting God in our image. Gender in the third person pronouns expresses sexual identity which is not proper to the transcending totally other. Sexuality is a limited otherness and hence a third person pronoun with a gender is not adequate for speaking of God, but it is the best we have. Man and woman have to speak to and about God within the limits of their language and understanding and our language will reflect our cultural standards and attitudes. Our use of personal pronouns certainly reflect a bias for male supremacy endemic in our inherited Greco-Roman culture. A contrived "he/she" does not compensate for the inadequacy of the pronouns and becomes a distortion of authentic sexual identity as if being male or female is to be only half human and half image of God. Human sexuality is in the image of God. God-she is as correct as God-he, but neither is adequate. We know who God is by knowing who we are. Our limitations in self-awareness and our cultural foibles and distortions about the human image will inescapably limit and distort our image of God. God talk should be comfortable. Our best God talk will always be in the second person in prayer but our Father/Mother will be pleased to hear us speak lovingly about him/her to each other in a single gender without affirmation or denial or concern about preference, inferiority or superiority but with the confident assurance that either and both sexes represent the total dignity and value of the human person and authentically reflect the image of God. To make gender an issue in our God talk misrepresents our human sexuality and confounds the issue and perverts the image. To assign sexuality to God is to cast God in our image, which is the ultimate idolatry. The question of whether or how to assign sexuality to God is inane and invalid. Because we cannot escape using a gendered personal pronoun in speaking about God, it will remain a choice conditioned by many factors. In this writing, God will remain the God-He who has been faithful and loving to me for a lifetime. The choice is a faith affirmation, not a theological statement.

1
INTRODUCTION TO THEOLOGY

FAITH IS NOT A RATIONAL CONCLUSION drawn from rational premises; faith is an experience of presence, a response to the benign presence of another which acknowledges the initiative of that other to whom faith is the response. Faith is a response of dependency and an experience of urgency—a confrontation with reality in which there can be no truce or neutrality. Faith is a decision for one's own identity. A believer is a searcher for whom doubt is anguish, and purposelessness is devastation. For the believer the truth is in sight to be touched, at hand to be grasped and in heart to be contained and possessed.

Today's believer is caught in the crossfire between his head and his heart. Today's believer has suffered the pain of inconsistency, the anguish of doubt and betrayal by false promise of proof and demonstration. Today's believer seeks credibility not proof and hears the promise of joy to the heart that is willing to search into the mystery that is God. The true believer knows that search for self and search for God are the same search. When we find God, we find ourselves in him; when we find ourselves, we find ourselves in God.

There is no arrogance in believing. The true believer is "poor in spirit," totally aware of total dependence upon God. The true believer possesses the Kingdom of God not by conquest or analysis, but by simply being willing to receive it. Much of what is called theology is not of faith. Many who are called or call themselves theologians are not really believers. We hope in this study to make a faith search into the theology we have known, not simply to test the adequacy of the answers that have been given, or the quality of the questions that have been asked, but to test the validity of the premises that have been assumed in asking the question in the first place.

If theology is to take its place credibly as a science and a discipline, it must assume full responsibility to establish and defend the validity of all its premises, and to keep all of its premises under constant assessment and reassessment. It is precisely at this starting point that much of theology has failed. In the first place, many of the premises of our traditional theology have been gratuitously assumed; the offense has been compounded by a claim of privilege and immunity for these gratuitously assumed premises. Theology has based its privilege on the claim that its premises are revealed by God, and its immunity on the claim that divinely revealed premises are in no way subject to human assessment. Traditional theology has likewise gratuitously assumed the conclusions of its companion philosophy as premises for theology and contrived a theology to fit these premises. It has further in effect gratuitously assumed cultural premises as divine revelation and that God makes revelation on these cultural premises. The primary example of this is the structuring of all moral and sacramental theology on the premise that the body-soul-faculty image of man and woman, as inherited from the Greco-Roman culture, is valid and adequate and is the image that God has revealed. These matters will be examined as our search progresses.

The primary function of a Christian theology is to make the Gospel credible in the culture in which it is believed and lived. For this reason, a theology is developed within the context of the culture of the believers who develop it and it is limited by the images and premises on which that culture is based. In our cultural history—as in others—theology has been the victim of cultural arrogance, the gratuitous assumption by culture and by theology that its premises are adequate to explain and account for all reality. In this study, we will consider the consequences of the arrogant philosophical and cultural assumption that its universal metaphysical categories can and do explain and account for all of reality. With this assumption, we end up denying mystery by explaining and defining it. Credibility for theology starts with the willingness to test, defend or assess any and all premises at any time. Theology is not the "Queen of the Sciences"—as has been assumed—with privilege and immunity because its premises are "revealed" but theology is "faith-ful servant" making the Gospel promise credible to those whose heart is in the search.

We have charged that there is fault and failure in the system; if the fault is in the premises, the whole system fails. We know that this is a serious charge with serious consequences. We will proceed by first assessing individual premises of the theology we have inherited, and after that, establish those premises on which a theology for our time can be credibly established. We hope to be fully responsible and accountable. Where we ask for change, we will put the burden of proof on the side of change and establish the credibility of new premises on merit. We will put any new premise to the test and let it rise or fall on its own merit, not by gratuitous assumption or authoritarian imposition.

In the beginning, we will cite examples of premises gratuitously assumed and implications of such assumptions in our traditional theology, all of which will be explored in this book.

At the trial of Jesus when Pilate cynically asked "What is the truth?" (John 19), he really didn't expect an answer. Our traditional theology is written on the premise that our cultural epistemology or criteriology is adequate and valid. We assume that what we call the truth is the truth, the whole truth and nothing but the truth because we have called it the truth. Our culture opposes truth to error. The Biblical Semitic culture opposes truth to lie. The gratuitous assumption of this premise that opposes truth to error has far-reaching and disastrous consequences. This premise puts the truth in the idea, not in the person, and the untruth is nothing but a wrong idea. Doctrine and dogma, not person, become the object of faith and the making of doctrine and dogma become the primary teaching function of the Church. If truth is opposed to error, making doctrine without error—infallibility—becomes the ultimate criterion of credibility. Every doctrine of the church—including the primary trinitarian and christological—is a theological conclusion, and as such, is no better than the premise from which it is drawn. It can be "perfectly logical," but not necessarily true. At best, propositions or theological conclusions can be only *about* the Christ. The primary teaching function of the Church is not to make doctrines about Him, but to present the man Jesus and His way of life to the heart rather than to the head of the believer.

Another example of the far-reaching disastrous consequences of gratuitous assumption of a premise is the unquestioned acceptance of the Greek image of man-woman as premise for moral and sacramental theology. The Greek image of body-spirit composite with faculties of intellect and will puts the truth in the idea, not in the person. We come to believe and accept as theological premise that we are "only human," with a pejorative "only." We interpret "Image of God" as *only analogous.* We reduce sacrament to the categories of causality. We presume an inner irreconcilable conflict between body and soul, because true to the Greek image, we say "We have a soul," rather than "We are spirit." We are forbidden by premise to believe the human spirit is the Spirit that is God, that man-woman is the best creature God has created or could create and still be creature.

We make God live and act in our cultural sense of time. We are ambivalent about this and try to cover our arrogance and error by making "eternity" of God an affirmation of endless duration rather than the "quality" of God's life. We adjust God to our cultural sense of time. We have God keep our past on the books unaware that our past is alive in us and in him. We give God a "window"—a moving moment between the past and the future which we call the present. We let God know the future, but if it worked the way we think it does, God's knowledge of the future would itself determine the future and there would be no room for God's freedom or ours. We try to reconcile God to our sense of time rather than simply put time in ourselves and put ourselves in God. Time itself is simply creation's way of belonging to God.

We have presumed that Greek universal categories are adequate to explain all of reality and, where these categories are clearly inadequate, we simply invent or contrive new ones. According to our premises, it is clearly not good enough to be "only human"; hence, we must be "supernatural" to be saved and we have created and contrived a whole "supernatural" order of being to provide salvation. The work of redemption couldn't be done by one who is *only human,* so we have contrived a "hypostatic union" and the categorical divinity of the Christ to explain how it could be and was done. Our premises preclude and exclude the immediacy and urgency of our interpresence with God. Thus, sacraments become intermediate and instrumental causes. Sacramental presence is confined to and limited by the hylomorphic theory of "matter and form," and the mystery of the Eucharist is contained in the categories of "substance and accident." We suffer from the disease of hardening of the categories. We inherit it with our culture. It is as epidemic as the culture. The more we are immersed in the culture, the worse the state of the disease. It becomes incurable when the last category is closed—the category of the absolute.

Questions opened at this point are not yet answered. They are mentioned here to make a statement of purpose for our work ahead. The questions opened are not an indictment of the tradition of Christian faith, but a statement of the inadequacy of *traditional* theology. The faith has been and remains constant and beautiful, but this present moment of faith calls urgently for new enlightenment. Faith calls for willingness to enter the mystery that is God with poverty of spirit. Faith calls for willingness to need and to be dependent, rather than to deny mystery by claiming to be able to define and to prove it. We can define and prove only those things that are smaller than we are. We stand with awe and reverence in the presence of the mystery that is God. In this study, we will enter the mystery with faith.

Faith will provide the criteria for this writing and reading. If anything in this book denies or reduces the glory of God, the integrity or glory of the Risen Christ, or if it denies or reduces human dignity or threatens the integrity of human freedom, then burn the book! On the other hand, if what is said here glorifies God, enhances the glory and the dignity of the Risen One, and if it enhances the dignity of the Image of God, and establishes the dignity of person and freedom, please believe it! There is nothing too good to be true.

2
PROCESS

HOW IT ALL COMES TO BE

GRATUITOUSLY ASSUMING THE ADEQUACY and total validity of our cultural premises boxes us into a narrow two-dimensional universe. We think we have a vision because we can see and count all the sides of the box that contain us. This is imprisonment of the soul in the body. Everything defined is doomed to the limits of the definition itself and everything proven is limited to the terms of the logic of the proof. In such a system, nothing, including God, can escape the limits of the categorical boxes into which we put God and his universe. Such arrogance is inevitably a self-imprisonment.

The principal offense is, in the assumed first principle, that all being is either substance or accident, that the universal categories of substance and accident are completely adequate and account for all of reality, including God. God would be un-God if there were anything accidental in him. These categories limit us to a two-dimensional universe. Substance becomes the ultimate substratum of all reality. In this system, substance is where all things begin to be, where all being is rooted. In this system, the truth is found in the substance of things; the substance of things is unchanging and change in substance would be annihilation. In this system, only accidents admit change, and hence, we have a perfectly logical fear of change and disdain for anything that can change. Immutability is canonized as the ultimate quality of real being, of truth and of God.

We must open our universe to a whole new dimension—process. Our old vision sees process as a series of changes that can happen only in the accidental and the changes cannot touch the frozen or fixed substance of real being and truth. Given these premises, historical resistance to the theory of evolution of the species was perfectly logical, because it threatened the universe and life itself with substantial change.

We must come to the vision of reality in which we do not say "the universe is *in process*," but rather, "the universe *is process*." We must say that process—not substance—is the substratum of reality, that the universe is process and that we are the people we are by getting in on the process that is God.

This requires a whole new way of thinking and speaking. In order to speak of this process that is God and the universe, we need a new vocabulary—at least we have to give a lot of old words new meanings. We must make language itself a process, not just a system of tagging ideas. In popular usage, our English is too static. Shakespeare would cringe at our attempt at elegance in making verbs from nouns by simply adding a suffix; the result is not much of a verb which should be an action word. How much better it would be to make nouns from verbs and to have nouns that retain the action of the verb. As a result of our usage, our God-language suffers.

In the history that we know, we are the first culture to ask the question, "Is there a God?" From the beginning of cultures the affirmation had been: "This is our God—who is yours?" As a result of our question, our culture has made the existence of God the first question and total issue, and have made the acceptance of the bare existence of God the criterion for being a *believer*.

Admitting or accepting that *God exists* does not make a person a believer in him. Existence is the least common denominator of all being and is the very least that can be said about anything and certainly the least that can be said about God. There is much more to say about God and to God than that he exists. The most that can be said about God is the affirmation and proclamation of *who God is,* and specifically *who he is to us.* A theology of who God is in himself is inane and is not theology at all. Whatever God is and whoever God is, is "God for other" and all that God is, is "totally other."

God for other, if not known by name, is really not known at all. Name is the identification of who and what a person is to us. Name is much more than a tag for identification. Name is the "word" that makes a person present. Name of God— name that is God—is at the center of the whole process of revelation. All of scripture is the faith process of naming God in an awareness of "benign presence," totally credible, demanding a total commitment.

Abraham is our father in faith because he leads us in the right search. His faith is not that God is "up there" or "out there," but "right here." God is where we believe in him. God is in his world for us, inviting and promising.

Moses, out of the faith tradition of Abraham his father, has the faith experience of the burning bush, the experience of a penetrating, encompassing benign presence that does not threaten or consume and destroy. His faith cries "Who are you, so near, so close, so present?" He receives the reply, "Your question is itself the answer, that's who I AM. I AM right here for you and for my people. My name is 'I AM here for you.'"

The name arrived at is not a rational conclusion but a faith experience constantly deepening throughout the Old Testament history of the people. Their human experience of fidelity and sin, of triumph and failure, of joy and sorrow, of life and death is the continuing revelation of "I AM here for you." In fact, they arrive at their deepest awareness of "Who their God is for them" from the bottom of the pit in captivity in Babylon. In captivity, in shame and failure, they became aware that God's presence was not vindictive but compassionate. Not only did they become aware as never before that they needed their God, they became aware that their God needed them to be his people.

How much better we could say "God" if the word "God" were itself an action word rather than a flat generic expression of an abstract idea that reduces everything that can be made "god" and all that God can be to a least common denominator. In our theology, we proclaim that God is one and only, unique, totally personally other, and then call on him in prayer with a word that can connote and denote anything from money, to perversion, to ultimate sin. We must not cop out by saying he is incomprehensible and ineffable. That would contradict and deny the whole creative process of revelation by saying the speaking God is not a very good speaker—especially when he speaks himself—and the speaking image of God which we are by being human is a caricature or a contradiction. If we have no image or a poor image of who God is, it is because we have no awareness or a poor image of what it means to be human.

Our human language has its limits and within these limits it can validly and even adequately speak God to those to whom God addresses himself. It is his language. Give the revealing God credit for being a good speaker and do not blame him for our failure or for our arrogance. Our greatest offense here is gratuitously to assume that our metaphysical categories are adequate to explain all of reality—including God. From that point, we proceed to put God into the categories of substance, person, nature. Once we assume these categories have *something* to say about God, we somehow assume they have *everything* to say about him.

The theological conclusions drawn from these premises become the object of our faith. We arrive at pompous conclusions such as this: in God there is identity of essence and existence and we consider this conclusion the ultimate achievement of human reason. If that were the case, our first and best prayer would be a cry or a hymn to the "Identity of Essence and Existence." I suggest we stay with "*Abba*, Father." God talks human. Revelation is simply the voice and language of believers affirming and proclaiming their awareness of who their God is to them. The simple experience of being human is the revelation of God—the deepening and expansion of revelation. The more we know about being human and human being, the more we know about God.

We who call ourselves Judaeo-Christians are one specific tradition of this faith experience. We look to what we call scripture as the record of the faith experience of our origins as what we are pleased to call the "people of God." Sometimes we make unreasonable demands on our forebearers in the faith in expecting mature adult experience and judgment from an infant people. We expect final words and mature conclusions from a people in the early stages of their faith search. At times, we do not let them speak their own language and we interpret their writings as if they were written last week in the language of our own everyday conversation. When we let them speak their own language and use their own images and allow them to be the Semitics they were, we encounter interesting insights about who our God is.

We lose much by presuming that we can translate all their language into ours. We cannot even translate their forms of the most common words, for example, the forms of the verb "to be." For the most part, we use this word as a simple copulative, a passive joiner, a totally intransitive verb. For them, it is a most transitive verb to be followed by the objective and accusative case. "I am me." I am your God (*Ego sum Deum vestrum.*) "You-are-my-son" is a creative word, not just an affirmation of existence and identity.

Besides making "to be" in all its forms the most transitive verb, we must also learn to make the word "of" more than a preposition denoting ownership or possession when speaking of God. The Hebrews have a usage called the epexegetical or explanatory genitive which is really not a genitive at all, but an affirmation of identity. "Love of God" does not mean the love that God has or the love that belongs to God, but means "the love that God is" or "the love that is God." "Is" is a transitive verb, the love that *"be's" or "is's"* God. The same goes for "Law of God," "Presence of God," "Power of God," "Compassion of God," and even "People of God," and "Servant of God."

In a previous paragraph, I used the term "human being" with a purpose, because it is the term that reduces person to the absolute least common denominator. A "human being" is about like an "H2O." It seems ridiculous that this term is canonized in a popular appeal for human dignity and freedom. "Treated like a human being," becomes the affirmation of personal well-being, relationship and dignity. We have heard "human being" as a synonym for person for the last time in this discussion.

Our purpose is to establish from observation and experience that our first premise is that the *universe is process*; that process—not substance—is the ultimate substratum of all being and reality and that person is the ultimate achievement of the whole process.

Every age is an age of faith in its own way. Every age is characterized by its primary faith premise. Every person in every age is a believer in his or her own way. Every believer-person is a searcher and every searching person must ultimately accept and settle for a premise that cannot be proven, a premise that is a premise only because it is believed. Even the cynic must believe and accept without proof that there is nothing to believe, and the agnostic must believe that nothing can be known with certainty. Believers in atheism are called unbelievers and believers in God are called true believers, but the god of many so-called believers is really not a true God and many believers in atheism are truly believers. Believers are identified and categorized according to what they believe, according to the object of their faith.

In our culture, we identify persons by the object of their faith more than by the quality and character of their faith. Many people who are called Christians are really not believers or Christians and many who are called "infidels or unbelievers" really are believers. Theology is about God, church and religion. Theology is a rational process working from rational premises to rational conclusions. These theological conclusions are statements and propositions called doctrines which in our culture become the object of faith in what we call religion; they are the dogmas or teachings by which a church and its believers are identified and named.

Because we make doctrine and dogma the primary object of faith in our culture, all believers, formally or informally, hold to something of a theological position, or have something of a theological basis or prejudice. Because their faith is so involved in theology and theology is so involved in their faith, theological positions and implications become supportive or threatening in the faith experience.

Believers in our time, according to the manner and object of their faith, experience three distinct fears and anxieties in their encounter with their culture, its movements and with the movement of contemporary theology. In our time, there remains much more than a residue of the classic fears of Pelagianism, pantheism and humanism.

In the public and private discussion of current theological issues, we encounter deep fears and anxieties on the part of many. Many feel threatened by much of what is said in light of new revelation and theological development. Many will say there is and can be no new revelation because they are trapped in the closed category of immutable and absolute truth and for them there can be no "new faith." Some are victims of their cultural and theological premise, that we are *only human*, and fear that we threaten and reduce the glory of God by making *too much* of His image. This is the fear of *humanism*. Then there are those who fear that when we make creation the real acting presence of God, we deny God's "independent" existence, somehow we have God contained in the things he has made, and that we make creation God rather than having God make creation. This is the fear of *pantheism*. There are those who fear that when we hold for the integrity of human freedom we deny or at least reduce our dependence upon God. This is the fear of *Pelagianism*.

As to humanism, the more that is made of the image of God, the more is made of God. He did not make a caricature or a *reasonable facsimile*. He made an image that proclaims the fullness of the glory of the Maker. All that God has to say of himself, he says in his image. It is the human faith responsibility to keep the image good enough for God. The classic humanist had the right question and had a reasonable objection to the culture, the philosophy and theology that insisted we are *only human* with the implication that it is bad to be human. Humanism held for the integrity of the human person and for the glory of being human. It is true that their answers and explanations in the old categories in which the issue was faced on both sides, were unacceptable to people of *faith*, and the *humanists* were thought to be *atheists*. Because the answer to the question was unacceptable, the question itself was authoritatively invalidated. Even asking the question became an offense against faith. That's a neat trick in a debate if you can get away with it. So far anti-humanists have gotten away with it. For the most part, *humanist* is a dirty name and *secular humanist* is completely anathema.

As to *pantheism*, the classic pantheist likewise had the right question, "How are all things into God?" The pantheist found that the traditional categorical answers removed God from creation, and made him only a *caretaker* after he made it, and he was right. The pantheist found that the old answers reduced God's real presence by making God's presence only a *reflection* in the things he made, and he was right. The pantheist found that a series of causality could not explain the phenomena of our experience in the universe and again he was right. Again the Pantheist's answer in the old categories, that all things are somehow *substantially* God is unacceptable in its failure to *distinguish* between God and creation. The answer is wrong, but the question is right; because we can't accept the answer, we may not invalidate the question.

The fear of Pelagianism has been around a lot longer. Augustine had his troubles with its author in the fourth century. It has been a problem in the history of the church that just simply would not go away. It figured strongly in the sixteenth-century Reformation and has lived on into our own time. The questions certainly have some validity and merit to have survived. Having been *officially* invalidated, attempts have been organized to ignore it out of existence, and have discredited it as being *heretical*.

The right question of the Pelagian was "How do we reconcile the integrity of human freedom with our total dependence upon God?" The answer in the old categories was unacceptable again because of a premise of faith. The answer of the Pelagian would simply be that in the last analysis and in the last instance in the process of human freedom, human freedom would have to be somehow acting independent of God in order to be free.

Before we go further, let us thank the Pelagian for refusing to let the question die, but to live on and to be opened up today as never before. The opposition to the very question can no longer get away with Augustine's answer *Mysterium est*—let us talk no more about it. It is still a valid question that cannot be invalidated by decree or ignored out of existence.

I have been, I am, and I will continue to be accused of *humanism, pantheism and Pelagianism.* Premises of the same faith, that validated the questions, will validate my answer. Note that I said, "premises of the *same faith*" not the "*same premises.*" We have to scuttle the old categories to realize that we had the answer all along, and really had the premise that validated the question of the humanist, the pantheist, and the Pelagian. The premise came from the ultimate Old Testament achievement of faith in *Yahweh.* In captivity and degradation, they became aware that their God, Yahweh, is "totally other."

If our premise is and remains "God is totally other," we cannot offend by humanism, pantheism, or Pelagianism. If we keep God "totally other," we know how to ask the right question. We cannot offend by humanism because the more we make of God, the more we make of man and woman, and the more we make of man and woman, the more we make of God. We can't offend by pantheism because the closer we bring God to us and us to God in a real interpresence, the more *other* we make him, the more we give him his own being, and give us ours. With the faith promise of God totally other, we cannot offend by Pelagianism because the more totally free we make men and women, the more dependent we make them upon God who makes them free.

We should remember that in these matters, we have defended our cultural faith in our categories more than we have defended our faith in God. We must admire the zeal with which the Pelagianists have defended their faith. Both sides could use a little more tolerance in the defense of the common faith in the same God. Our God, who is Father of our Lord Jesus Christ, and raises him up in glory in us, really doesn't care that much about what we call him as long as we call.

The fact remains, that the highest revelation of God is that to be God is to be totally other. Accepting the existence of God or accepting God's total otherness as a theological premise does not constitute belief in God. Belief in God is a self-movement into the interpresence of the totally other. It really says more and says it better to say, "I believe in God when God becomes my God. I have love and life going with my God."

There are constants in all that's going on. Our first premise is: *PROCESS, not substance, is the substratum of all reality.* The world is process; time is process. Our concept of time comes from our view and experience of process. Concepts of time vary greatly from culture to culture. The more the concept approaches pure process the more authentic and meaningful it becomes.

Many ancients had a cyclic view of time. They observed the return of the sun, the moon, the seasons, the cycles of fertility, etc. They were trapped in the cycle in which everything and even human events seemed predetermined. The cycle was deterministic and closed. There was no way to escape the cycle.

As stated in the introduction, our cultural concept of time is *linear*—past, present and future. The present is but a fleeting moment—the *"nunc fluens"*—the flowing now, a thin and tenuous, almost imaginary dividing line between the past and the future. This is affirmed and reaffirmed by a myriad of aphorisms about the fleeting present moment and the fleeting passage of time. Our past is back there, irretrievable, gone forever, even gone out of existence. What is past is no more and will never be again. From the insecurity of the present moment which already has become past since your reading the word, we look to an unknown future *out there* which is threatening precisely because it is unknown. Aphorisms again tell us that the past is gone, and not to count on the future; there is no way to be sure of it. In this sense of time, neither the past or the future really exist, or they exist only in the mind or memory of God.

The Semitic culture, out of which the whole Bible is written, also has a linear sense of time, but quite different from that of the Greeks. For them, the present was the permanent establishment and presence of everything that had gone before. In fact, everything had not "gone" before; it simply had "come" before and here it is now. The future is likewise coming to the present. It is not unknown, unmade out there in the dark threatening, but it is breaking in on the present. It is simply God. The urgency of the present is to make something of the future when it comes. A prophet did not foretell the future, but he told how to read the present to meet the future. Trying to reconcile God and human freedom with our sense of time has been a great source of anxiety and an unanswerable challenge to faith in our whole world history. We have tried to put time into God, because we could not put God into time without denying him. The results have been disastrous. God doesn't have to enter time. Time is simply the continuing "God to other presence" in the universe.

The sense of time becomes an important and even a determining factor in human behavior. The stimulus for human behavior is always a "present" experience, but never isolated from the "past" or "future," whatever that may be. The present likewise is in continuity with the past into the future. How this happens and what it means is a sense of time.

The sense of time varies from culture to culture and even from person to person within a given culture. The sense of time becomes a criterion for much of the value judgment of the person and the culture to which the person belongs and is a significant element in any cultural heritage. (See Graphs A, B.)

Person is process; church is process; sacrament is process; spirit is process. In process nothing is ever left behind. In the process, there is continuity of identity without interruption and as the best constantly gets better, the best is always more of the same. Process reality and truth is *to other*, never *in itself*. All things and all people are what they are to others—no more, no less.

An internal system or series of causality alone does not work. It cannot account for the best getting better. A cause cannot produce an effect greater than itself and causality alone would trap us in the law of diminishing returns and not only would the best not get better, each effect would be less than its cause. For example, causality cannot explain evolution.

In reference to other of the same kind being the most important element, it is interesting to note that as life forms develop, sexuality appears as a creative othering to the same kind. In the process, the higher the life forms become, the more hetero (other) sexual they become. It is further significant to observe that there is no other life form as completely heterosexual as the human form.

ANCIENT CYCLIC SENSE OF TIME

In primitive cultures time encloses and contains. The future is only a return of the past time. Cyclical time is deterministic and holds freedom victim and captive because there is no power to determine the future.

GRAPH A

GRECO-ROMAN SENSE OF TIME

PRESENT

PAST	PRESENT	FUTURE
—irretrievable, gone forever, "only a memory"—moving away	—a thin dividing line between the past and future—a fleeting moment from which the past is receding—somehow entering a future that doesn't exist until the present enters in.	—out there—unknown and threatening but bound to happen.

BIBLICAL SENSE OF TIME

PRESENT

PAST	PRESENT	FUTURE
—simply everything PRIOR to what is now present—moving toward and arriving at the present	—where it is all together, total and permanent estabishment of all that "has been"—the whole past brought forward—nothing left behind, meeting the future.	—the becoming present—moving toward the present—inviting and promising—not threatening unless the present is evil.

GRAPH B

Heterosexuality in the process is a work of perfection, a level of excellence, in *to-otherness*. We should not speak of two or even opposite sexes. We should say there is sexuality which is the dynamic of the otherness of the male to the female, female to male, by which male is not whole without female and vice versa.

The completeness of human heterosexuality is unique. It pervades the whole being. There is nothing "unsexed" or neuter about being human. Man and woman have so much with which to be other to each other. Homosexual persons certainly have a lot to be other to each other, but heterosexuals have a lot more. We must become more aware of the corporate dimension of heterosexuality and God will not need to be *he* or *she*, but *our God*. (By the way, women are currently far ahead of men in achieving this corporate awareness.)

It really says more and says it better to say, "I believe in God when God becomes my God. I have love and life going with my God." If the God of a woman person is totally other, God would be God he; for the man person, God would be God she. I do not know the total implication of this, but I am certain that sexuality in God's human image has a lot to say about our totally other God of whom we are the image.

In the cosmic process, *awareness* constantly deepens from atom to spirit in continuity without interruption in an othering process in which our origin is our destiny. *Othering is our origin*; arriving at the totally other is our *destiny*. In any stage of the process, we are what we are to others—no more, no less, and what we are to others we are to God.

Concerning premises old and new, adequate and inadequate, we spoke of establishing the premise for general awareness and for theological process, that ours is a three dimensional universe in which we say "the world IS process" rather than that the "world is In process." Time is the experience of process. Process is itself the ultimate substratum of all reality, where all things begin to be. This requires and deserves some explanation, but it is utterly simple and so utterly profound that it is not all simple easy.

Graph C indicates that all is process and process is all, that it is many, but that first and last it is one, but all is different, yet all is the same in creation. All is good and is process, which is simply, the best is getting even better. Our origin is our destiny. That can be graphed in the image of an upward thrust. Each unit in the graph is an image of each and all of the others, and each is contained in all of the *others*, and all of the others in each. Reference in size is not comparison of importance, but somehow an indication of the levels and stages of cosmic process. There is the atom in the human brain and the human brain is in the atoms that make it up.

Our graph will take us from the atom to the human brain. We start with the atom because it is somewhat familiar ground for all of us. We are not affirming that the atom is the beginning of the process. We simply break into the process at the level of the atom fully aware that so much has gone on to bring about the fusion of the atom with which we start.

The atom is not the container of its parts—nucleus, proton, neutron, etc. The atom is nucleus, proton, neutron being to each other. Its dynamic is "*to other*" and this "*to other*" dynamic is creation itself, in which the whole cosmos with the human person, the Risen One, "*the first born of all creation*" is totally other to God.

Otherness becomes atom to atom, molecule to molecule and at each new level of otherness becomes a *constant*. Note in this process, we don't look for absolutes and we reject the limits of the absolute, but we see the *constants*. Our first constant noted here is that others of the same kind are always the most important factor in the cosmic environment and in any environment. How few of us have ever seen an H_2O. There have to be many of them being other of the same kind to each other before there is what we call water, and being water is not a static accumulation of a lot of H_2O's, but a dynamic intransitive

What's going on...
CONSTANTS:

• Process not substance is substratum of reality.

• Nothing left behind—atom gets better and better.

• Continuity without interruption (vs. fixed species)— same, but more and better.

• Dynamic of "to other" reality as against "in itself."

• Best gets better vs. causality and law of dimishing returns and effect always less than cause.

• Environment deepens and broadens.

• Others of same kind always most important element in environment (heterosexualtiy).

• "Awareness" constantly deepens—from atom to spirit in continuity without interruption.

• Origin is destiny.

• Graph starts with atom, presuming fusion—a lot of process has gone on before the atom came about.

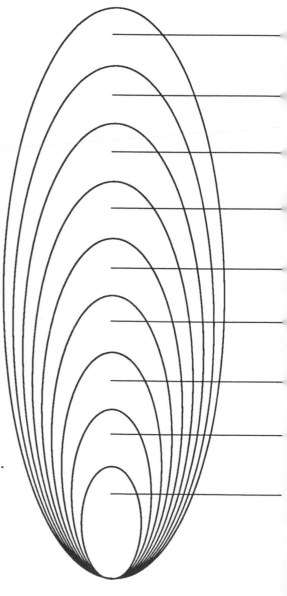

GOD
TOTAL PRESENCE TO OTHER
THE ULTIMATE "TO BE TO"

Human life—spiritual—enter morality, introspective self-awareness and responsibility for other, enter also integrity of individual—contains every other level at its best, e.g., best atom, best H2O, etc., in human brain—whole universe becomes environment for spirit—spirit "belongs"—ultimate heterosexuality—belonging to each other to the whole universe.

Gregarious animals more individualized—no strangers—corporate awareness—"to the herd, for the herd."

Higher animals, more individualized, more hetero sexual *animal behavior.*

Enter sensate—lower animal colonies "to each other" (biology).

Higher forms—trees-forests-praire-tundra-sea (botany).

Enter life—carbon-oxygen-bacteria, etc. (biochemistry).

Molecules to molecules-to elements-mineral world before life there is color-sight-sound-form. We see molecules and cells of same kind together—we don't see a H2O or an alga.

Atoms to molecules—atoms remain atoms—only more so—affinity physical "laws."

Each atom itself a process—particles responding to each other make the atom.

GRAPH C

be-ing to each other which *be's* water doing all its things. There is water in the stagnant pool, in the primordial swamp, which is the same water which constitutes eighty-five percent of the human brain. But water in the human brain is water at its best. Molecules become the whole range of what we call elements and because they are "to each other" and really are all of the same kind we have light and color, shape and form in endless *to other* meetings. We have mountains and sky, landscapes and moonscapes, to be brought to endless *to otherings* by the *to othering* creative presence of the artist, the composer, the architect, or the homemaker boiling potatoes for the family meal.

Elements in *to other* harmony invite and call forth a new level, which is the continuity of the best getting better in coming to life. It is not the introduction to *something else, from somewhere else*. The "world comes to life," not just because the elements, such as carbons, oxygen, etc., are there to sustain it and maintain life. The cosmic thrust demands it. It has to be. The chemistry of elements become bio-chemistry, more of the same, the best cannot do anything but get better.

To other of the same kind remains the dynamic and becomes more so than ever, and is no longer only a *culture* of bacteria, or the scum that is algae in the stagnant pool, but it has become trees and forests, prairie and tundra, sea and sky with endless forms and ways *to other* in the level of life whose mystery we try to penetrate in what we call botany.

Process produces the next level, sensate life, whose mystery we try to penetrate in the science of biology. Our scientific search and experience has been the ongoing revelation of mystery and each question answered opens a myriad of new questions. Each penetration of mystery simply expands and deepens the mystery. But the *to otherness* is not only constant but is constantly deepening in the phenomenon of endless forms of life and ways of living. The *to otherness* of ecosystems and bio-ecosystems, and even the *to other* necessity and balance in these systems of forms and species of life that appear at first glance to be destructive and life threatening to each other are really the dynamic and the harmony of life itself.

From *to other* colonies of ants and swarms of bees, we come to herds and otherwise named *to other* groups of animals that are models of harmonious *to other* interdependence of the individual upon the community and the community upon the individual. This interdependence provides maintenance, support, and total benefit and biological excellence and integrity of the individual and community.

When in the process human life emerges, it is out of this gregarious awareness that there comes the self-initiated, self-awareness that is uniquely and distinctly human. All awareness, heretofore in the process, has been somehow a physically determined response *to other* of the same kind and to the myriad of stimuli in the *to other* environment. Now we have the dawn of self-initiated response, the dawn of human awareness, the beginning of the question of identity, which is still the human question of urgency today. Perhaps, we have come a long way in answering the question, but we still have far to go.

Coming out of the gregarious herding and even family-*to other* awareness that characterized the best that had so far appeared on the life scene, as always, the best got better. All creation is *to other* related in the becoming image of God who is *totally to other*. An "I am" humanity could not have *belonged* in the *to other* world that *belonged* to it. The first and proper human awareness would have been "we are" not "I am." The Genesis story of origin certainly seems to put Adam and Eve, Mr. and Mrs. Everybody, into a *to other* garden. To arrogate to self the "knowledge of good and evil," is sin precisely because it denies dependence upon God and others. Thus the sin of refusal to be person *for other* is expressed in the complaint, "Why should I be my brother's keeper?"

The point of all this is that biology, anthropology, archaeology and even history attest to the primacy of the corporate, that the first thing about being human is that we are a corporate person. It is the authentic natural human process. There is no real human achievement without it, and all sin is violation of an interpersonal *to other* relationship. All virtue is virtue by creating other.

In the cosmic process, everything comes together and is at its best in the human person. H_2O is at its best in the human brain. The whole cosmic awareness comes together in human awareness, which is the spirit capacity of self-initiated response, "*we are to other*," "*we are to you.*" We get in on God's "I AM" as our own and in him "be's" the whole universe and especially *our own kind* is our other.

For our premise, we are not proposing an abstract concept, but a living existential awareness of being human. We are proposing that creation is the on-going cosmic process. God is constantly, totally creating, not just adding increments moment by moment, day by day. Because we are being constantly totally created, we are constantly totally dependent, constantly receiving our total being from God.

Cosmic process, ultimately becomes person, and person is process capable of self-presencing in the image of God. Hence, a person being person is a *to other* presence in the image of the *totally other* God. In creation, the tree is God-Word made tree and the tree and all created things don't tell us *about God*; they are God present speaking himself to all other but especially to us, who by being in his image and responding to him with a self-initiated response, are other of the same kind to him. In the process, the resurrection is the ultimate creative presence of God and the ultimate human response. The resurrection is the present moment of creation and the church is the present moment of the resurrection. Process becomes person who can presence; *to other* presence is sacrament or symbol, the substance of another chapter. Hence, our title puts it all together *PROCESS-PERSON-PRESENCE*.

3
BIBLE

LITERATURE OF THE PEOPLE OF GOD

WE HAVE SPOKEN OF THE ORIGIN and the writing of scripture in the process of human culture and human society. In the same process by which the writing that speaks for the people of a given time in history and culture became the classics of that period, the collection of books that we call the Bible are the classic literature of the People of God. We are created in the image of God. It is in what we are, what we do and what we say that God speaks himself. He speaks to us by speaking in us.

The Bible is not an exception to this creative speaking process. The Bible comes within and out of the process in which we are being created. God does not create us and at a later moment begin to speak to us. All creation is the speaking and what is being created is the Word. What we are as human being and being human is Word made flesh, the speaking presence of God. We are the revelation of God.

Now the question in our own language is, what is the immediate object of our learning? Does the Bible tell us who God is by telling us who we are, or does it tell us who we are by telling us who God is? The Bible tells us who we are, and by truly knowing who we are, we know who God is. The Bible is the affirmation of self-awareness of the People of God. It is the affirmation of the faith of the corporate person from infancy in the desert to resurrection from the tomb. The person born of faith and promise in the desert has come to identity and a growing adulthood in our resurrection. We have a lot more growing, learning and affirming to do, but now we know who we are. We are the Risen One and in all our growing, learning and becoming, we are becoming more that person. We have scarcely begun to see our glory, but when it is fully achieved and fully revealed, it will be the fullness of the Christ we now know ourselves to be.

The immediate communication of the Bible is human to human. The Bible is in a totally human situation; it is as human in origin and in process as any other literature, but it is fully and authentically human. That is the uniqueness of the Bible. It is fully and authentically human as an affirmation of identity. It is written and spoken without deceit or lie. It is spoken from the whole spectrum of human experience in moving from origin to destiny. It speaks the pains of birth, of the growing pains of a people. It speaks of struggle and failure, of achievement and success, of joy and sorrow, of fidelity and infidelity, of crime and punishment, of virtue and reward. The message is constant. "You can't go wrong by believing in God. You can count on him; he keeps all his promises for those who are willing to risk believing in him." This God doesn't promise happiness in an afterlife but happiness and joy in the present life. For those who believe and find this joy, the afterlife is no issue because this joy is so great it simply has to be forever. The beautiful thing about the promise is that the joy is not a reward for putting up with being human, it is the experience itself of being human.

The Bible is our own faith experience. It is not a source of faith somehow outside of what and where we are. Its *inerrancy*, *infallibility* or whatever else we may choose to call its authority, is not its superhuman or supernatural quality, but simply the integrity and fullness of its humanness, the integrity of the human faith from which it is born. The Bible itself presents the Christ out of the process of its own origin. He is born of faith, the other circumstances that otherwise are the least of human origins. He is nurtured by faith and he is the Christ and we are saved because he is the total believer who went to his death for others believing in his Father's promise of resurrection. To believe in him is a self-movement by which we become that man and get in on his faith, not that he does our believing for us, but that he is the first believer and so he stands as the Risen One.

The process is one; the Christ comes to us and we come to the Christ by the same process as the Bible comes to us and we come to the Bible. It is the process of faith by which God comes to us and we come to God. The Jesus did not require a special protection, a supernatural guidance, a position of privilege or special powers. With any of these he would not be "Word made flesh" which affirms that his true humanity is his integrity. The Bible in its own unique way is "Word made flesh." Its "flesh" is human words spoken by human persons, and the Bible is true by the integrity of the faith of the speakers and the bearers of the Word that it is.

It would be and is an arrogant presumption for any person, institution or "authority" to set itself up as competent to judge the integrity and the truth of the Word and the work of Jesus by comparison to any criteria whatsoever or even to judge whether or not such and such is truly a Word spoken by him. In the presumption of such authority or competence, there is always the arrogation of superhuman, better than human power, to protect us from being *only human*.

There is a great deal of this arrogance on the part of any "authority" that presumes to validate the Word and the work of God by presuming to set the criteria and standards of truth and performance for those who believe in the Word and do the work of God. The Word of God is the believing people and their faith is the greatest work of God.

The Christ and the Bible come to us in the same process. They are one and the same speaking presence that is Word made flesh. Unfortunately, we have divided, separated and made the Old Testament Bible to be a story *about* the people of God and the New Testament Bible to be a story *about* Jesus, which are somehow *sources* of our faith *about* the people and *about* Jesus. Whereas, the Bible is the living speaking presence of the believing people of God. In our Roman Catholic tradition, we have placed an emphasis on *tradition* also as source of faith. While our theology of *tradition* has for the most part been a kind of an arrogant assumption of exclusive authority, the Catholic Faith in tradition has been a very authentic awareness of the process by which the Word comes to the ongoing present moment of faith.

In this, we are aware of struggle of good and evil, confrontation with culture and confrontation within culture. In some cultures, the confrontation is truth versus lie; in our culture, it has been confrontation of truth versus error and heretics have been burned at the stake, not because they lied about the Christ but because they made a mistake as judged by cultural and institutional criteria. There has been charge and countercharge. There has been division of families and of nations. There have been wars and persecutions, all about what we think the Word of God is and what it means.

In our own time, there are the same "Holy Wars" in the pulpit, in the classroom, in the press and in all the media of public communication. The process is the same. Every believer needs a prophet and even the prophet needs a prophet. The prophet's prophet in biblical times, throughout history into our own times, is the need of the people of God. Our first concern is to discern and to find the true prophet. Finding the true prophet is always simple, but not always easy. The first requirement for the believer is to recognize his or her own true need for the Word of God and acknowledge that the Word is always received from other—to acknowledge total dependence upon God. The believer must realize that faith is a decision and the believer must accept the responsibility to make his or her own decision, not to seek the comfort of having someone else make the decision for him or her. Any prophet who claims the authority to make our decisions for us, any prophet who promises instant salvation or who promises easy religion is a false prophet. On these criteria, we can exclude a vast horde of the contemporary false prophets that bombard us with their messages. A further criterion, more difficult to discern but always discernible, is what in our culture we call motivation. Is the prophet truly concerned about the real human needs of all the people or does he or she exclude groups or classes of a given people, or whole peoples or races from his concern. Today's prophet must be very conscious of classes, but the true prophet cannot be *class conscious* and exclude any class or group from the mission of care and concern.

In this matter, the primary horrible example is the exclusion of women from the prophetic role of preaching and ministering the Word of God. Paul, the true prophet, had to make the agonizing decision to "leave his own people" and carry the Word to the Gentiles whom "his own people" would have excluded. In his letter to the Galatians, he proclaims the universal prophetic mission of the gospel where he says, "There can be neither Jew nor Greek, neither slave nor freeman; there can be neither male or female, for you are all one in Christ Jesus." (Gal. 3/28.) Today "Jew or Greek" has become Jew or Gentile and expanded in exclusion to become also, white or black, Oriental or Western, Caucasian or non-Caucasian, even Catholic or Protestant. Slave or freeman has become upper or lower social or economic class and male or female not only remains, but has been exaggerated as an issue of exclusion.

Women have been excluded from full membership in the church and society, first and most of all, by the cultural premise of male dominance and male supremacy. This cultural institution of feminine inferiority has been reinforced by a history of exclusion by rigid social, governmental and ecclesial structures and practices, all of which in their exclusion are the instruments of preserving the status quo of the false prophets.

The only possible logical premise for the exclusion of women in the prophetic role of preaching and ministering the

Word would itself be an impossible contradiction of the Word and the fact. This premise could be only this: that women are in fact inferior as believers in the Word and that, in Christian sacramental identity, they are less baptized than men and this is the only possible logical reason for their exclusion.

The facts are quite the contrary. The facts deny the premise. In today's church, women are at the leading edge of faith. Women are achieving an awareness of corporate person and an awareness of the feminine spirit in the image of God. Women are speaking with a prophetic voice. A prophetic voice always calls for a decision. And women are speaking the real issues of the moment. Women are in the forefront demanding decisions for justice, human dignity and human freedom. The prophet is out front, an immediate first instance speaker of the Word in a situation of urgency.

The other side of the process is the faith response to the prophetic Word. There, too, women are out front in listening and hearing and discerning the Spirit that speaks the truth. Theology is part of the discernment process. There are many very credible women theologians whose insight and feminine logic open dimensions to faith heretofore unknown and unheard in our culture. It is really not a new discovery but a return to the biblical sense of prophecy and to prophetic logic.

Logic is the process of arriving at new truth. Our culture is trapped in its own logic. Our culture knows only the rational Greek philosophical logic, which is the logic of ideas and quite logically excludes any other logic as fallacious. The logic of the biblical prophet is the logic of events which a rational logic of ideas can explain only by foreknowledge or a knowledge of a future event before it happens. Hence, our popular cultural image of the prophet is one who foretells the future. The prophet sees and reads the present; the prophet interprets the present and simply sees and says where it has to go from here. Prophets often are unpopular because they have to speak out against the cultural and popular view of present events. One such present event is the emergence of women theologians and scientists, etc.

All of this is said simply to identify something of the present cultural and sociological environment for the prophet and for the believer. This moment has never happened before, but there are constants here from every other historical and cultural moment of prophet and believer. There has always been a Babel of confusion of speakers, but there is the ongoing pentecost of a truly prophetic proclamation of the Word in one tongue heard and understood by all who are willing to believe. The Bible always has to be proclaimed and believed as a present speaking, not a record of a past event. Hence, it is not a matter of why wasn't that question asked before, but by what arrogance does a present prophet or believer presume to answer a question that wasn't answered by the best minds of the past.

A good example of the question and the confusion of a given historical moment is the current question of the "sexist" language of the Bible. The Bible is written by believers for believers in a given historical-cultural living context of language spoken by prophets and believers. Verbal languages vary from culture to culture, in manner of speaking, and especially in the image of man (there we go again) from which the language is drawn in the first place. Our English language is one of the many languages that gives gender to personal pronouns and it is the language that is very "sexist." Our culture itself identifies a person first and most by sex. A child is born and we ask the question, "What is it, a boy or a girl?" After that first question, there is no more room for it because it is so terribly neuter. We can't say person it, much less can we say God it. Hebrew doesn't have that pronoun problem to begin with. The Hebrews could and did very comfortably attribute feminine qualities to God. In fact, the best thing that the Old Testament faith learned to say about God was feminine. When they arrived at the high point of faith awareness that Yahweh their God was totally other, that is their deepest awareness of who they are to God and God to them. God to them was constant in his compassion and care. You can always count on him. The best thing they could say about who God is to them is proclaimed in feminine images. Their God is compassion, a God who even suffers with them and comes to love them as never before, and never before have they been so loved. The scripture speaks of this abiding love as *Hesed rechemim*, "the constant love of the wombs of God." The plural here is not numerical; it is the Hebrew idiom for emphasis. If the best they can say about their God at his best to them is the feminine image, they should not be accused of "sexism," which is not contained in the Hebrew affirmation of biblical faith. The Hebrew Bible, however, does reflect the patriarchal structure of society and cultural institutions which was the context in which it is written and, in spite of that contextual limitation, it proclaims that God is *totally other* to each person and to all peoples.

In the same manner, there is never a vocation in scripture to any one person or people to the exclusion of any other. All people were called in Abraham. The call to favor and privilege for the Jewish people was for all people. The promise made to them is fulfilled in the gospels. Emmanu-el, God is with us, is everybody's name. The promise is constant, universal and faithful. Our concern must be about the limitations and failure in bringing about its fulfillment rather than faulting the promise because of the limitations in the language in proclaiming it.

Every age has its own questions yet unanswered, and every age has its own answers to the old questions. Every question answered opens new questions. The prophet doesn't promise to have all the answers, but the true prophet can tell where the answer lies. The true prophet can invalidate the wrong question. The true prophet hears and respects the right questions but most of all the true prophet assures the believers of the benign constant saving presence of God and invites the believers to enter that presence by being willing to risk taking him at his Word.

4
LIBERATION THEOLOGY

THEOLOGY AND FUNDAMENTALISM

IN OUR TIME, we have become deeply aware of the connection between our sociocultural inheritance and our social and individual behavior. How much our behavior is determined by inheritance and the extent of the influence of the sociocultural genetic package on our behavior is a fascinating question for the moralist and for the behavioral scientist and sociologist. Our purpose here is to observe and to examine a theologico-cultural phenomenon and somehow to trace this phenomenon to its cause and origin in our cultural premises.

We have noted frequently the categorical nature of our cultural premises. We have observed that our culture gratuitously assumes that the universal ontological categories of our basic cultural philosophy are completely adequate, that these categories can and do account for and explain all of reality. Beyond that there is the more subtle gratuitous assumption that thinking and speaking in categories is the only way to think and speak. Then there is the further assumption that all speaking and thinking is categorical and in our own established categories. We must remember here also that when we assume that our categories are adequate, we also assume that they are mutually exclusive. Those that are perfectly and totally logical in taking our cultural premises to their perfectly logical conclusions are what we are pleased to call Fundamentalists.

In our cultural compulsion to think and speak in categories, we note differences more than sameness, and we identify and define by differentiation. It works and it has its own validity, but it is not the only way to do it, and really not the best way to do it. As a prime example, let us take what our culture and our theology has done to the image of man. Man and God can't go into the same category so we have reduced "image of God" to analogous with God and have removed man from presence, to distance, etc. Racism is categorical thinking emphasizing minor differences even to the exclusion of transcending sameness.

We bring this same kind of thinking to our political, social and religious issues and we find it easy to identify and name our groups and categories with names and epithets that not only identify by differences, but that also reflect our judgment about them.

This is true also in religion and in theology. We have *liberals* and *conservatives*, we have *old* and *new*, we have *modern* and *traditional*. Then we have "Liberation Theology" and I would name "Fundamentalism" as the opposite number. Liberation theology says we must move on. Fundamentalism says by no means, we got it made where we are. Liberation theology says we have new questions that demand new answers. Fundamentalism says all the questions have already been asked and we have had all the answers right along.

Relatively few people are aware of the dimension of the confrontation between fundamentalist and liberationist and very few are at all aware of the confrontation and conflict that is shaping up, and is already going on. Probably, the deepest and most significant unawareness is that we are unaware of the deep entrenchment of fundamentalism in our culture and of how fundamentalist our entire theological tradition really is.

It is a situation where people who are in fact fundamentalists are using *fundamentalist* as a pejorative epithet, the stove is calling the kettle black. Fundamentalism is the cultural and logical process of taking our cultural premises to their logical conclusion. Somehow, we don't call it fundamentalism until the conclusion is reached and at that point those who hold to the conclusion, we call fundamentalist.

The Council of Trent was the triumph and canonization of fundamentalism, validated and made completely respectable by Vatican I with its doctrinal definitions of the infallibility of the church and of its Roman Pontiff in matters of doctrine and dogma. The Council of Trent was a fundamentalist answer to the Protestant Reformation. It stated the doctrinal position of the church and condemned the doctrinal position of the reformers. The council of Trent drew the battle lines and the church assumed a "siege mentality" of being under attack from the "gates of hell."

In the gospel, Jesus says to Peter, "You are Rock." In this name and image, Jesus speaks of the person quality of a living faith, not a fortress under attack. The "gates of hell" are under siege, not the church. The church is on the attack and mounting the siege not the "gates of hell." In the image the "gates" are the last defense; when they are broken down, they do not "prevail." "Will not prevail" is not the failure of the attack, but the failure of the defense. Our counter-reformation theology has put the enemy on the attack and the church on the defensive in a ""siege mentality." The primary thrust of theology has been "apologetic" or defensive. It has been primarily a civil war, allegedly over doctrinal issues, but really more the issues of the authority to make the doctrine than the doctrine itself. For four hundred years, the battle lines have become more firmly established with a no-man's line in between and the war goes on until recently.

On the horizon within the view of both sides, a new enemy appears that is common enemy, a radical threat to the total Christian tradition. The gospel way of life is challenged; all that Christianity stands for is threatened by injustice, by conspiracy of power, and evil in high places. It comes clear that the alleged reformation issues have become totally inane. We should long since have listened to Pogo rather than to our self-styled seers and have come to the conclusion that in the Reformation battle "the enemy is us."

Today's ecumenism agrees with Pogo, "the enemy is us." Ecumenism is not a theology; it is a movement of the spirit—a movement of faith. It is a liberation movement in which theology will not validate the faith movement, but the faith movement will validate the theology. Again, there is a confrontation in which "the enemy is us." Fundamentalism calls ecumenism heresy, compromise, relativism, infidelity and even blasphemy. There is, however, a great hope that this not degenerate into typical post-reformation in-fighting but a convergence of energies of the Spirit. There is hope that we will find our common faith in the saving presence of our Father in the Word made flesh and that Jesus says what he meant and meant what he said when he spoke the good news and that our differences are only in our theology, in what we think that word might mean.

While we hope for more light and less heat in the intra-cultural, inter-denominational movement to a transcending ecumenical vision, there remains a highly visible formal and informal theological confrontation between liberation and fundamentalist theology.

In our culture and especially in our Roman Catholic tradition, being a fundamentalist gains more respectability, and even becomes a virtue in our cultural premise about *authority* and obedience. Our cultural image of the perfection and virtue of *blind obedience* is very fundamentalist and serves as a good example of the process. In fact, our culture has distorted the image of blind obedience and made it a caricature. *Blind obedience* in the origin of the term meant that the obedient person found the person in authority could be taken at his or her word without searching or looking further, hence, blind, no need to look. Blind obedience was simply comfortable, confident faith in the word of a loving and caring authority. Our fundamentalist culture demands proof, and is satisfied only with demonstrable measurable premises and conclusions. Obedience is not the unthinking conformity to *law and order*. Obedience is the vision of faith, the willingness to risk accepting a promise and the sense of urgency to achieve the vision and to bring the promise to fulfillment. Of course, this presumes that law and authority gives a vision and makes a credible promise.

Our *law and order* culture has come to the point of saying it is right and good because the law says so. It is true because the church says so, it is true because God says so. The process of revelation and of faith is to establish the credibility of God and the prophet. This is first, and the believer comes to believe in the prophet who doesn't make things true by saying them, but says them because they are true. A thing is not good or right because the law says so, the law says so because it is good and right. The laws and teachings of the church are not right and true because the church says so, but the church says so because they are right and true.

We are well aware of the fundamentalist interpretation of the creation story as taking place on six consecutive calendar days preceding the first Sabbath. Fundamentalists interpret the scripture as a kind of an isolated absolute existing entirely outside of any real existential human context. The Bible is something we mysteriously have in hand, that has been put into our hands by its own initiative, that it comes from God to us without us. The most and the best that we do in the origin of scripture is entirely passive. Fundamentalists do the same for Christ and the church.

On the other hand, the Bible is a human achievement in response to and totally dependent upon the divine initiative. The Bible is human literature, most of it of very human quality. If the Bible were visual not verbal art, the fundamentalist would say the word is done in its own medium, something so unique that no other work but the Bible is done in that medium and that no other work can ever be done in that same medium. It would be said that it is a medium that needs no interpretation, that it is somehow its own interpretation, a kind of unique artistic medium that speaks for itself with the same total message for everyone that admits of no individual difference. Fundamentalism says that we are given the meaning directly, that the medium is not a medium at all. If there happens to be any variation in interpretation from person to person, it can be only because someone is at fault or in error.

For the fundamentalist, the scripture in its origin comes before faith, whereas, in the process, the faith of the people is the origin of the scripture. It is the literature of the people of God. Fundamentalism denies the total human dimension of the origin of scripture and denies the context of human experience of history and culture and in effect says it is literature without context. In this way, in insisting on the divinity of the Word, fundamentalists deny the humanity of the Word.

Denial of the humanity of the Word of God has dire consequences for power and authority that claim to act and to speak in the name of the Word. Such power and authority frequently arrogates divinity to itself and we can have as a result an Islamic terrorist government or an Ecclesial Spanish Inquisition in the name of God.

Fundamentalist denial of the humanity of the Word has other dire but logical consequences. For the fundamentalist, especially in our culture, anything and everything human is *only human*, and all human effort and achievement is doomed to failure. The human world is without hope, an evil world that must be endured and ultimately escaped. For fundamentalists, it is a world from which we must be saved, and salvation becomes a rescue mission in which we are snatched from the fiery pit or from the teeth of the dragon.

Finally, fundamentalism is not limited to religion but carries over into social, political and economic affairs as well. In these affairs, it performs in the same way that it does in religious affairs. It proclaims that we already have all the answers and that there is an easy answer to all possible new questions in the answers we already have, that things are as they are by the will of God and that theological conclusions become premises for political and social science. In mixing and confusing the disciplines of theology and political science, they invalidate the separation of church and state on the authority of the Word of God and impose fundamentalist religious premises on everybody as a requirement of the political science which they have just invalidated. Fundamentalist religion can lend respectability to repressive governments and to programs and policies that deny social justice. Right wing dictators don't repress fundamentalist religion. Oppression from the radical right is as offensive as repression from the radical left.

The scriptures are a common property that is shared not by division but by each person's total possession. The Bible belongs totally to each believer. The Bible is sacrament of the speaking presence of God totally open to every believing person. The Bible is unique not because it is somehow superhuman in its origin or its message; it has the same origin and comes to us in the same process as any other literature or art. Its uniqueness is that of being the literature of the people of God.

In other literature and art, we speak first of appreciation and then interpretation. When we speak of interpretation, it is for the purpose of deeper appreciation, to open the reader to everything the literature is saying, even constantly to find new meanings and insights. Appreciation and interpretation of literature would never start from the premise that the writing or art piece has a fixed content.

That the Bible has a fixed content is exactly the premise of the fundamentalist. Such a premise, first of all, presumes to place a limit on the working of the Holy Spirit. The Holy Spirit is the human spirit, the human possession of the Spirit that God is. All the work of the Spirit is *for other* and *to other; its for otherness* and *to otherness* is the work of authenticity. The *to otherness* of the Word spoken or written is an inviting presence and openness to be heard, seen, taken possession of and entered into intimately and personally.

The faith reading, listening and hearing of the Word that is the Bible is a living response to entering into the speaking presence of the believer that speaks or writes it. As in the human interpresence and communication that is achieved in any other speaking or writing, the first requisite is a sense of urgency to respond and to enter into the experience of the speaker, writer or other artist. This urgency is faith, an expectation of a new creative experience. In literature and art, the true teacher will tell the student what to look for and how to look for it, but will also direct the student to *believe* that the work is a promise of real value, of joy and of creative personal experience. The most important part of teaching appreciation is to bring the student to faith, to come to believe in the artist and their art and that everybody's response is authentic.

Appreciation comes before interpretation and interpretation should bring about deeper appreciation. Art and literature are open to all. The gallery and the library receive people at all levels of competence in appreciation and interpretation. To exclude any person or any group, viewing or reading, would be a grave injustice and an obscene affront to dignity and freedom. To make the art and literature the exclusive property of a privileged few is not only an injustice to those excluded, but an insult to the artist and his work. The only set of rules for the gallery or library is to create and maintain an environment conducive to appreciation and interpretation of the work. There will be posted no set of general rules for appreciation or interpretation for all of the works, or for the works individually. People of all levels of competence in appreciation and interpretation will pass by in endless procession with a real and deep individual and community experience of intimacy and communion with the artist—an experience that transcends time and space.

The Bible is a gallery, a collection of the *works* of the best believers in our faith tradition. For us, it is an in-hand possession available to any believer. There must be no exclusion by specific rule or by implication of incompetence like a gallery posting the rule "admission limited to professionals only," or "admission limited to tours conducted by official interpreters." In the history of the church, some rules have, at times, been somehow posted excluding people from the Bible, but most of all, there has been and there still remains exclusion by implication and inference of incompetence, and the Bible, somehow, has been and remains "for professionals."

In reading the Bible as in the experience of any art, appreciation comes before interpretation. We have put so much emphasis on content and interpretation that we have excluded and discredited *appreciation* as unworthy and somehow beneath the dignity of the Bible. We have held that *appreciation* really has nothing to do with faith.

Anybody who appreciates the Bible has a level of faith; his appreciation is his faith. Without faith, there is no appreciation. Appreciation without faith is a contradiction. However, competence in interpretation without faith is not a contradiction and in our history, we certainly have had professional interpreters who have not been believers.

We must, first of all, learn the value and admit the validity of appreciating the Bible. Appreciation is always the first response and is always an authentic response. In western Christianity, the Protestant tradition has generally fostered appreciation and until recently, the Catholic tradition has, at least implicitly, downgraded and discouraged it on the allegation of the incompetence of people. Fundamentalists not only discredit appreciation, they exclude it entirely from the experience of the Bible. Fundamentalists hold that the Bible has a fixed content that in no way admits the factor or dimension of varying personal experience in reading it, because the fixed content determines the authentic response.

The Bible needs appreciation even more than interpretation. The Bible invites the total human response, and the more totally authentically human, the deeper and richer the response in faith. We must not exclude feeling, passion, emotion and imagination from our faith response to the Word of God. Our total response includes every human energy at its radical source and in its deepest movement.

God honors us when he speaks to us. He speaks covenant. In covenant speaking, there is no question of greater or less, superior or inferior, equal or unequal. The offer of covenant is a total unconditional offer of self to other, total other to total other, inviting a total response. The response is worthy only when it is total, that is, totally human.

Fundamentalism excludes totality by not admitting appreciation. The premise of fundamentalism is that we are *only human*, and that the human dimension of feeling, passion and emotion are sinful and unworthy and would defile the "purity" of our faith response if permitted to enter. The premise of Liberation Theology is that to be human is to be good enough for God and that everything truly human is worthy of God. Sin is simply failure to be human; sin is refusal to be good enough for God. God's Word is worthy of God by being worthy of us, right for us, spoken for us as being worthy and dignified and that it is right that we are in his image. We must not sin by denying the scripture any of its human dimension thereby discrediting God as speaker of the Word by failing to put his Word fully, completely and totally understandable in the language that we are, by being human. Good enough for us is good enough for God.

5
BELIEVING
IN CONTEXT

MORE THAN DOCTRINE AND DOGMA

EVERY BELIEVER AND EVERY STATEMENT or profession of faith is culturally colored and conditioned. Often the culture dominates the faith and the resulting statement is more of an affirmation of cultural premises than a profession of religious faith. The culture becomes the religion and God becomes God in the image of man, rather than man in the image of God.

The process of believing and professing our faith in our own culture has been particularly susceptible to this fallacy. We must constantly make difficult distinctions and separations. Revelation is a continuing event in a real living cultural situation and event. In fact, the event itself in its cultural setting is the revelation of God. God is always revealed by and in the people who believe in him. The Bible is written by believers for believers. This believing people's profession of faith in their God is revelation. The Bible itself is an affirmation of the ongoing event of a people believing in their God.

The historical background of the New Testament scripture is spoken of as the Christ event. We should not speak of the Christ event only as the individual life, death and resurrection experience of an individual man from Galilee and as a past event from which we draw residual benefits. Rather, the *Christ event* is the ongoing church process. The church is not the result or the effect of the resurrection. It is the ongoing event of the resurrection in the body that is the Christ. The resurrection is a cosmic-creative-established presence that has drawn mixed responses and mixed reviews. The resurrection is primarily the creative presence of the Father raising up his son/daughter in us. The church is the total human response to the resurrection presence and promise. Generally in our culture, we have insisted that the resurrection be on our terms in our images. We have not only insisted that God be cast in our image, but we have arrogantly set the limits and the criteria for the affirmation and proclamation.

We have made the formulary proclamation of doctrine and dogma the primary "act of faith" in our culture and history. Faith is not the rote proclamation of a common formula by throngs of people or the public acclamation of a vested cleric in the view of millions by media coverage. Faith is an ongoing corporate commitment of the people of God to the gospel way of life with the expectation of the fulfillment of the gospel promise of joy in the very living of it.

We tend to isolate the "act of faith" from its real living existential context and to examine it in an intellectual vacuum. Faith comes from faith; faith engenders faith. Faith is a gift of God from other believers. Faith is belief in God when and where he reveals himself. Faith does not come by a pipeline or a hot-line from above as fundamentalists believe. In living reality, the only way to come to faith in God is to believe in a person who believes in God. That person also has come to faith in a person who believes in God. The chain of believing persons goes back to Christ who himself has come to faith by believing in persons, who believed in persons who believed in God, back to Abraham, the first believer and father of our faith tradition.

"What do you expect?" can be a cynical question but "What do you expect?" can be a valid question in any situation that demands faith. There is more sin against faith in expecting too little than in expecting too much. To expect the church to make doctrine and dogma without error is expecting too little. To expect the church to preserve the text of scripture without error is also expecting too little. To expect the church credibly to present the man Jesus and his way of life and to expect that way of life to be joyful and fulfilling is to believe authentically in the word of God. To take him who is the Word at his word is to be a believer after the heart of God.

If we are truly to listen, to hear the word as we *read* it, we can say as we *listen* it, we must be attuned to the speaker. That speaker is a living believing human person, who speaks a human language, in a real present existential human condition and human situation.

In the past, we spoke of the various "senses" of scripture and the text became a kind of *Deus et machina* to suit the purposes of the interpreter. "Exegesis" became *eisegesis* which is a process of reading meaning into the text, rather than the art of distilling the meaning out of it. In this process, the interpreter would determine which "sense" applied in a given text. The "sense" became a kind of magic formula for determining the meaning. This issue was settled once and for all in the encyclical, *Divino Afflante Spiritu*, written by Cardinal Augustine Bea for Pope Pius XII. The encyclical, which is the "Magna Carta" for biblical study, is an instruction on the interpretation of scripture. It establishes and protects the integrity and authenticity of the biblical text, and it establishes the freedom, the rights and responsibility of the interpreter of the text. *Divino Afflante Spiritu* affirms that there is only one sense of scripture and that is the *literal sense*. Here *literal sense* does not mean what we might think. To discover the literal sense we have to make a search into the real situation in which the text was written. Every such situation involves two persons, a speaker and a listener, both of whom are believers. (In scripture and in all speaking of the word, the "Word is made flesh" and the believing person is God speaking.)

In American English, we use the word *literal* as opposed to *figurative*. We use the expression "to speak literally" or to "speak figuratively." In this usage, *literal* comes to mean real, exact, precise—implying the impossibility of misinterpretation.

In contrast, we will say another statement is "*only* figurative" and, "if only figurative," leaves room for doubt or misinterpretation. "If only figurative," it lacks precision and is not the kind of language to use for saying important things. In this usage, we use the word "literal" to denote the manner of speaking—*how* it is said—with no reference to the meaning. That's simply the way we use the word in our culture, the way in which it is understood, and the first meaning we give it.

In *Divino Afflante Spiritu*, however, Cardinal Bea speaks and writes in a different language in which the word "literal" does not mean the manner of speaking or writing. "Literal" for this document does not refer to *how* it is written, or *how* it is said, but "*What* does it mean?"

In searching for the "literal sense" of scripture, we must ask this question: "What did this believer-writer intend to say when he wrote these words?" The answer to the question involves many further questions such as "Who was this writer?" One thing that every writer of scripture has in common with every other writer is that they are all believers in their own way. Each writer believes and writes in a particular and peculiar set of circumstances and with the urgency of that unique moment and event.

In writing the gospels for instance, each writer retained his unique, individual character and personality, and each author drew from his own unique sources. In what language did he write? What was the urgency or the need of the time of the writing that he was responding to? What problem or question was he addressing? Given some level of answer to these questions we can begin to interpret something of what he meant to say when he wrote the gospel. This is not a different problem than that which we have in interpreting the Constitution. What did the founders intend to say when they wrote this article and what does it mean today? It is likewise true for literature. What did Shakespeare mean to say when he wrote his words? In interpreting the Bible, the Constitution or Shakespeare, the process is humanly the same. It does not mean that we are contriving and making meaning for the words. It means we are searching to find the meaning. Faith in the Bible is unique as is the Bible itself. We believe in the Bible, we believe in the Constitution, and we believe in Shakespeare. Because we believe, the search goes on. It is perfectly valid in a constitutional issue to ask, "What did the framers have in mind when they wrote these words?" "How are the words to be applied in our moment?" Because they didn't have or know public schools in the sense that we have them now does not mean that the Constitution has nothing to say about public schools today, nor does it mean that it has said everything about public schools. Likewise, contraception was not a social or moral issue at the time of the writing of scripture, but that does not mean that today when birth control is a front-line social and moral issue that scripture has nothing to say about it. Neither does it mean that scripture has said everything about the problem and has passed a final judgment.

To believe is to have expectations. A reasonable faith has reasonable expectations. One error is to have unreasonable expectations from scripture: that scripture has said everything about everything, that it has the answer for all the questions that can be asked, and that it precludes and excludes any new questions. The Bible does, however, speak of an ascending order in the creation of the universe and is certainly open to what we would speak of today as an expanding universe. The Bible precludes a Godless universe. It precludes life without purpose and a universe without design. The Bible simply has the premises of faith of the people that wrote it. The constancy of these premises of faith is what we speak of as *tradition*.

We are in the tradition of the faith of Abraham. The sciences of history and archeology have determined the date of the Abraham event to be about 1850 B.C. This does not mean that about 1850 B.C. God chose Abraham and began to speak to him and that this is the beginning of revelation. The very creation and millions of years of the process were themselves revelation. God creating and God revealing is the same God doing the same thing. Creation is revelation; revelation is creation. God had been revealing for millions of years. In Abraham, he finally had a believer. The Bible does not say that Abraham was the first believer there ever was. Genesis 14/15 has no problem accepting Melchizedek, a priest of the Most High—contemporary with Abraham—who didn't get his faith from Abraham. The Bible simply affirms that Father Abraham is the first believer in our faith tradition. Our Bible is the symbolic, real, sacramental presence of the first believers that wrote it. (See chapter on sacrament.) The biblical literature speaks the faith experience of the Abraham-through-Christ-event, and in the writing, credibly establishes that event in the stream of human history. The prophets didn't write. Jesus didn't write. Believers in the prophets and believers in Jesus did the writing. The Bible is the symbol-sacrament of their faith experience. In reading-listening the Bible, we get in on their faith experience.

The Bible and tradition are not two separate sources of faith. Tradition is the ongoing process of a people believing—the process of a believing people. It is the process of the human spirit, the process of continuity of identity, the process of affirmation and proclamation of identity: "Yahweh is our God; we are his people."

In the process, it is most important to note that Yahweh our God wants to be known in no other way than as the God of the people who believe in him. The Bible is a manifestation, a kind of phase in the ongoing process that is tradition. The Bible is the human response to the presence of God. This does not reduce or remove "Word of God" or God's speaking presence. It is simply the way God speaks. God talks human; God's speaking is "Word made flesh." This "Word made flesh" is not an aggregation of individuals, but a corporate person with a continuity of identity as a person from Abraham through Christ into us. We tend to break the continuity by dividing this "Word made flesh" from the person that we are and in whom we have continuity of identity as person from Abraham through Christ.

In the process of remembering and remaining aware of our origin, we tend to reject and disclaim our provenance as people of God. When we speak of Old Testament, we tend to make a separation, not only *Old* and *New* into our categories of *old* and *new*, but also to insert our whole human history into our cultural sense of time. *Old* and *new* in our usage somehow become mutually exclusive with the *old* becoming irrelevant and, if not discarded, somehow stored away in the attic.

In this creative revealing process, we do not *descend* from our ancestors in the faith—we *ascend* from them. It is a person process in which nothing is left behind. Everything is brought forward. In our experience in being adult person, our infancy and youth are not just a memory or a trace of the past. Infancy and youth are present not only as effect of the causes operative upon us *back there* and *back then*. Our infancy and our youth are alive in the organic living structure and living awareness of who we are in the urgency of this living moment. Our infancy and youth are of the presence that we are right now. If the living presence of the experience of my being four, five, and six years old were somehow violently removed from me at this moment, I would be terribly confused and cut off from my own origin. I would become a person without a childhood, because in losing my fourth, fifth and sixth years, I would also be losing my first, second, and third years. I would be separated from my origin, and even the years after six would be confused and troubled.

By our treatment of the Old Testament, we have tended to do just such violence. In spite of our disdain, the Old Testament remains with us as the faith experience of our infancy as the people of God. Old doesn't mean gone-by or no longer relevant, or displaced by the new. Old means young. It simply means prior in the process, but still here, alive and well, in the continuity of identity of the corporate faith person that we are. In our infancy as faith people, we read the benign presence of God in our experience of a nurturing, sustaining, promising presence in the world about us. We read the experience of the wonders God works and the favors he does for a people who risk believing in him. We have come, perhaps, to early childhood and adolescence in a fuller vision of what it means to be his people, his daughter-son, being raised up in glory as the resurrection people. Perhaps, we are beginning to see our adulthood, but our infancy is also now with us as a real experience. The faith person who found God in the desert is the person who has found him finally and fully in the tomb. We have come to the point of discovering the tomb as our origin, but we have much more to discover about what it means and who we are as a resurrection people. Do we believe John 11/25 which says, "Everyone who lives and believes in me will really never die." We are even afraid to say this in our ordinary rendering of the text and in the way we speak of death as absolute and final.

All of this has many other serious implications. It provides answers to the burning questions: "Who are the Jews?" and specifically, "Who are the Jews to us Christians?" The name *Jew* has come to mean many things, but first of all it should mean that they are the people-person that we are. This is not because we share a common human nature, but because they are *us* when we were born and when we were young. They are our infancy and youth alive in us. In fact, we can't be fully alive without them. The Jews are not simply a historical phenomenon that somehow mysteriously, persistently survives in spite of continuing threats and attempts at extermination. Without the living survival of the Jews there is no survival of the people of God. They must survive in their unique identity as people-person of our faith origin. The Jews are the living presence of our birth, infancy and childhood. The Jews are not just a source of our Christian doctrine content that we have borrowed and taken the credit for preserving. The living Jews are the living presence of our faith origin from God. When asked the question, "In what language is the New Testament written?" our answer should be, "The New Testament is written in Old Testament, the language of our origin and childhood, even though first proclaimed mostly in Greek signs and symbols." The mind and the heart and the spirit of the New Testament scripture is Jewish simply because it was a Jewish faith-person who wrote it. That faith-person proclaimed it in Greek, because Greek was the cultural language of the people to whom it was being proclaimed in the writing.

Jews being Jews is a religion, not a nationality, and their religion involved the development of a religious literature which we call the Bible. While there did develop a sense of an "official" and approved list of those books which belonged to the collection called the Bible, the Jews were open to let the collection of books develop and grow and to let the text itself develop and improve. They did not think in any way that God had spoken his final word and there was no more to be said.

On the other hand in the Christian tradition, we have had the urgency to close the list and freeze the text on the premise that all revelation is closed with the death of the last apostle. This has been compounded in our cultural process in which Christians are mostly culturally Greek, and thus the Bible teachings become rational premises. In the process, we have developed a body of doctrine by rational conclusion. These doctrines have become the object of faith. Difference in doctrine has become division in religion. Consequently, the Christian body has been divided into warring sects.

In the last twenty years, however, there has been a remarkable agreement among the sects about which books belong to the Bible and which is the most authentic source and text, but we remain divided about what we think the text means. In short, we arrogantly insist that our rational conclusions drawn from the text are more important than the sacred text itself. We

denial. Thus it happens that in the Jewish Christian telling of the story and affirmation of their authentic Jewish origins, the "Disciples of Jesus" became the good guys, and the "Pharisees" became the bad guys and were blamed and condemned for the death of Jesus. Remember again this is contextual and as context, it is neither affirmation nor denial as the word of God. The contextual dimension of the Gospel of John should not be used by Christians as a "gospel" condemnation of the Jews, nor should it be used by Jews as evidence of an anti-Semitic Christian proclamation. In the context, it is not Gentile Christians bad-mouthing the Jews, but rather Christian Jews bad-mouthing their Pharisee Jewish brothers and sisters. The Gospel of John did not just happen to be written, but as any other book of the Bible, it addressed and answered an urgent need of its time.

No matter how the death of Jesus came about, the death scene in John's gospel presents an answer and calls for reconciliation. The presence of John and Mary at the foot of the cross not only tells of Jesus concern for his Mother and the courage and faith of John to be there, but the scene calls the whole Jewish community to witness Christ's death. The whole Jewish community is there. Mary is Jewish Mother, the Mother of Christian and Pharisee. John is the Christian community. Jesus says to the Mother Jewish community, "This Christian community is your son", and He says to John, the Christian community, "This Jewish community is your Mother." "And from that hour the disciple took her into his home." The people who wrote the gospel had the memory of John's care for Mary in his home within their own community, but it seems that the division in the community was so bitter and deep that it has never been healed.

We have mentioned often that the faith of the people of God is the source and human origin of the Bible, the Word of God, and the faith of the people is the "keeper" of the Word of God. To "keep" means more than to "conform to." We keep the Word like we keep a promise, a friendship, a garden. We nurture and make it come true and bring its promise to fulfillment. All of this happens in the process of the human community of believers. In the process, some strange things happened. Unreasonable demands have been made on scripture with unreal expectations. But overall, the Word and the work of God are self preserving and self validating and are the ultimate constant and promise and presence of everything we need to live for, and everything we need to live by.

The Word of God, however, is not the Word of God until it is believed by those to whom it is spoken. God is not God in himself or God as such. As God is God to other so his Word is *God-speaking-to-other*. We have God's Word today from believers in the word. Faith is not a series of believers, but the process of an ongoing present moment of response to the Word. In the creative process we have to become more and more human. To achieve a more authentic humanity in the "*building of the body who is Christ*," we must become more human. There have been moments of glory; there have been moments of more modest success and moments of failure. There have been even moments of denial of the Word. It is our responsibility to make ours a moment of glory.

Original sin is not just a bad moment in the past, but original sin is a *glitch* in the ongoing process. It is sin at origin. As we are constantly at our origin, receiving the Word in a constant process, there is sin constantly to be overcome in our response. There is also human limitation. Limitation is not sin nor is limitation a failure. Limitation is simply the human condition of total dependence. Without limitation we could not be loved or spoken to by God, but in being loved and spoken to, we become the lovers and speakers for God. This is the process in which the Word comes to us and will come to others. Isaiah speaks of the process when God says, "The Word that goes from my mouth will not return to me unfulfilled, before having carried out my good pleasure, and having achieved what it was sent to do." (Isaiah 55/11) A moment of failure simply delays the final return.

What is our present moment? It cannot be denied that it is a moment of great faith, a moment of search, a moment of great urgency to hear the Word and to proclaim it. When there is such a moment there are always prophets and false prophets. There are those who, like Jeremiah have the urgency to proclaim the word at any cost. There are also false prophets whose word is their own lie proclaimed for their own aggrandizement. At such times, we must remember more then ever that the Word and the work of God are self-validating.

We must also remember that in scripture, God does not just condemn the false prophets but most of all condemns the people who believe in them and give them their power and their security. There can be no prophets, true or false, without the people who hear them. People who hunger for the Word of God will recognize and hear the prophet of God. People who search for pleasure, power and false values will hear the false promises of the false prophets. Believers make the prophets true or false. To blame the false prophets for our troubles is like saying, "The devil made me do it." There are always those who will hear what they like to hear and there will always be those to tell them just that.

The final responsibility is always with the believer. It is *believers* who make the people of God not their prophets. Believers make the church, not the structure of authority that governs or speaks with "authority." Every believer has to have a prophet, whoever or whatever that prophet may be. A true prophet is a believer, and even the prophet needs a prophet. The people of God are the prophet's people. The experienced needs of the people are the prophet's prophet. The true prophet has concern and compassion. The prophet cares for his people and brings the healing Word of God to them by experiencing the urgency of their need not because the prophet is authorized by *proper authority* and comes through proper channels. As Word of God the true prophet needs no official authorization, because the word of God and the work of God are self-validating. The word and the works of the false prophet are self-deceiving and self-destructive.

When people are ultimately destroyed, it is always self-destruction. People will always get what they really believe in even if it isn't always what they expect. In fact, when a people are free to determine their own destiny, they will always get what they deserve. People tend to seek the comfort of having someone else make their decisions for them. They tend to elect leaders as prophets to speak *to* them, but the prophet they choose will ultimately always speak *for* them. Hitler was elected by the people to be their prophet, to tell them all the things they wanted to hear about their destiny as a super race. Hitler spoke for them. The flawed character and madness of Hitler did not destroy them. The people's faith in the false prophet destroyed them. The people chose their prophet in the image and false promise of what they wanted to hear and what they wanted to be and become.

In our day, the technique of the false prophet is image making and image projection. The tools are at hand to make and project images massively and effectively. There is the massive production of the image of the carefree, debt-free-comfortable upper middle class family that people vote for in the market place and in the polling booth with the confidence that poverty and injustice can be ignored out of existence. Before Nebuchadnezzar destroyed the city of Jerusalem and the temple, false prophets told the people that they were *standing tall* and were invincible because they had the "temple." They never had it so good. They ran Jeremiah out of town and the city was destroyed. Every great empire in the world has fallen at the moment the people became convinced that they were invincible. (Note: Amos and Osee in the Northern Kingdom.)

Prophecy is not a phenomenon and a process only for the temple and the church. Whether it is called "religion" or not, whole nations and individuals will live or die by the prophets they believe in.

Prophecy is always at work. Every person is a believer and every believer has a prophet who is taken at his word. Etymologically the word "prophet" means "a speaker for." God's prophet is a speaker for God. The criteria for judgment about the truth of God's prophet are these: if what the prophet says glorifies God and declares our dependence upon God, if what he says proclaims human freedom and responsibility in the image of God, the prophet is true. If the prophet exalts human reason above God and evades or ignores any human responsibility for others, or responsibility for our own decisions, the prophet is false. Every prophet is a promisor. Every false prophet promises instant fulfillment. The true prophet will have to say that fulfillment will take some time, or a lifetime, and that you will have to clean up your act first, before the promise will come true. The true prophet will have to say that you can't ignore or back away from the message. You must pay the price. No false prophet, or even the devil himself ever says, "I am against God." The true prophet says, "I am on God's side; join God." The false prophet says, "God is on my side; join me."

The false prophet promises easy religion and instant salvation. The false prophet makes an image appeal to the affluent not in a crass promise that power and wealth can buy salvation, but that it is a sure sign of God's favor. The prophet Amos says, "Listen to this saying, you fat cows [cats] of Bashan, living on the hill of Samaria, exploiting the weak and ill-treating the poor...the Lord God has sworn by his holiness. Look, the days will soon be upon you where he will use meat hooks to drag you away...." (Amos 4/1-2)

Another image and false promise is that salvation is found in vast throngs, in a stadium filled to overflowing, in a crowded, elegant and glittering temple, with vested choirs and flowing robes, or in the vastness of a milling crowd striving for a glimpse of a traveling religious dignitary. Again hear God saying in Amos 5/21, "I hate, I scorn your festivals. I take not pleasure in your solemn assemblies."

We have a false assurance of safety or salvation in numbers without any real sense of the primary human corporate personality, of the primacy of corporate salvation, or any real sense of corporate sin. We think that one plus one equals a real worshipping body by accumulation and that corporate sin is somehow likewise accumulated. The result is that we call ourselves a religious and even Christian nation by reason of the numbers that "go to church." Self-righteously, we declare ourselves sinless because the people that "go to church" are not in jail; our churches, auditoriums and stadiums hold a lot more people than our prisons and jails.

In all of this there is always a prophet out front, on the podium, at the microphone or at the end of the procession on his way to the podium. Numbers or press notices, statistics, or a host of press agents do not validate the prophet. Acceptance and approval by the crowds or by the general public do not validate the prophet. The word and the works of God are self-validating. The true prophet is a true believer who is willing even to risk his life in letting the word of God speak for itself, while the false prophet arrogantly claims that the word of God proves that the prophet is right. The responsibility and decision, however, are ultimately with the people. Acceptance of a false prophet is always self-deceit.

The Bible remains a constant prophetic presence in human and cultural history. The Bible is a constant speaking presence, constant symbol and sacrament of the faith of the person who wrote it and the person who believes it. The Bible is not a third party, or an instrumental cause. The Bible is a speaking presence, an affirmation of the faith identity of the people of God. It is an affirmation of our origin which never becomes past. We are constantly being born in the desert and from the tomb; we are always the living, spirit-breathing people of the ongoing living moment. For this reason there is no final interpretation, no once for all apodictic definition of meaning. To attempt to define the word of God involves the same arrogance as attempting to define the mystery of God. The "WORD IS GOD," and any attempt to define this mystery is an implicit denial that it is a mystery.

Hence, there is an ongoing search. Theology is an aspect and a dimension of the search. The Word is always spoken by a prophet. Theological research and speculation can be prophetic and, as in all prophetic utterance, the believer must make the discernment between the true prophet and the false.

The fact that in our time we will observe and identify contextual errors in the assumption of the cultural premises of the theology of another age is no more a condemnation of the prophetic affirmation of that theology than noting that the context of the Old Testament is unscientific, or non-scientific. The fact that we observe contextual errors of traditional theology is not a denial of its prophetic affirmation anymore than observing the contextual errors of the Old Testament scripture is a denial of the prophetic affirmation of the Word of God.

Difference in theological opinion from age to age, from culture to culture, or from person to person is difference in what the Word of God means to us. The most important thing here is not the statement of a definition about the meaning, but the fact and affirmation that it is meaningful. Our affirmation that the Word who is God means everything to us, must be our affirmation of faith that we mean everything to God who is totally other. "Lord we do believe, help our unbelief." (Mark 9/24)

6
SYMBOL AND MYTH

LANGUAGE OF FAITH

TO SET THE STAGE OR THE TIME for the discussion of myth and symbol, let us paraphrase another summary statement from one with the authority to set the stage for all human endeavor. "Therefore, I say to you—a new commandment I give unto you; never say *only a symbol*, and the second is like it; never say *only a myth*."

Note that we have reversed the usual of "myth and symbol" to "symbol and myth." Symbol comes first because symbol is *THE PROCESS*. Symbol is the creative process of establishing transcendent permanent presence of person to other—*PROCESS, PERSON, PRESENCE*. Myth happens in the symbolic process.

All language is symbol, but there is a peculiar *language* for symbol itself within every language. Our culture and hence our language really aren't good at symbol because *only a symbol* is a part of the *only human* syndrome of our culture. The commonly accepted meaning for the word *symbol* is something unreal and a contrived substitute for reality, with the common question "Is it the real thing?" or "Is it only a symbol?" The same goes for myth: "Is it the truth, or is it only a myth?"

We have the words but not the language. The word *symbol* has the same Greek origin as the philosophical categories that have caused such havoc. They have been considered adequate to explain mystery and presence of God. Etymologically, symbol is an action word from the Greek meaning to thrust or throw together, to put elements or things together with purpose, design and energy. We will keep it as a good word to name the process of person presencing self to others with urgency, immediacy, at the deepest level of the experience of being human and of interpresence with others.

Our language, as well as all languages have the verb "to be" in all forms necessary to affirm existence and reality as it happens to be seen by the people who speak the language. It is a common presumption that "to be" means the same thing in every language with different sounding words. This couldn't be farther from the truth. The verb "to be" with all its tenses and moods—used in the tenses and moods as auxiliary to other verbs—is the best indicator of all cultural sense of time, which is also deeply involved with our sense of symbol or lack of it.

In our language, the verb "to be" is mostly simply copulative, intransitive, a joiner of subject and predicate and many times makes an even stronger affirmation when it is omitted entirely. This is especially true in Latin. "*Deus ineffabilis est.*"

In our language for symbol, we will borrow from the Semites for whom all of the forms of the verb "to be" are transitive verbs. By the way, this will help us read the Scripture, all of which was originally written with the transitive "to be." See what this does to God's "I am"—"I am your God"; "You are my people." "God" and "people" are in the accusative or objective case or "I am the way, the truth, and the life" would become and should be: "*Ego sum viam, veritatem et vitam*". (Excuse me, non-Latin readers. This can't even be said in English.)

"I am" would come to mean "I be me." We have some dimension of it in the imperative form: "You be quiet,"—"be good." "Be my friend." In casting into a role we say, "You be Hamlet," or "You be right field." Transitive "to be" not only opens the whole world to the process of "being to other," but simply includes everything in the process and brings our whole world out of two-dimensional substance and accident, etc., into the expansive third dimension of process.

We are suggesting that "*other*" become a reflexive transitive verb. In our common usage, it is mostly an adverb or an adjective that denotes, "not the same," "different than," "different from." We say "other than," rather than "other to." We need a process word, and our word "other" in our common usages has beginnings for such a word. We need a word that speaks self-movement, a word that says "otherness." Otherness is all that we mean to each other, that by which we do mean something to each other. The "*total otherness*" of God is that by which God means everything to us, and wonder of wonders, that by which we mean everything to God.

I have just written "of process" in a previous chapter, "Introduction to Theology." We borrow again from the Semites and their case of what the grammarian calls the epexegetical genitive. The genitive case in our language denotes possession or ownership or control.

I don't know who did the counting but it is said that in ninety-eight percent of the times that the word "of" is used in the Old Testament, it is used in the epexegetical genitive. And we use the word "of" to denote the same thing. "The people's right" has the same meaning as "the right of the people," and "God's law" is the same thing as "the Law of God."

In our English (and Latin and Greek) rendering of the Scriptural text, we use the word "of" for the genitive case to translate the Hebrew "epexegetical genitive." For the most part, it becomes a possessive genitive. "Law of God" as *epexegetical* really means much more. "Epexegetical" means *explanatory*. It is the affirmation of the identity between the two terms. "Law of God" means "Law that is God." The same goes for "Love of God," "Compassion of God," "Presence of God"—and it goes all the way—"Word of God," "Son of God," "People of God," "Church of God," etc., and etc., "Word that is God," "Son who is God," "People who are God," "Church that is God." At this point I hear the cry, "That is blasphemy." The more sophisticated will cry, "Pantheism." Others will cry, "Humanism." It is simply symbol.

In the first place, we must remember that our categorical cultural premises not only can't explain symbol in the real sense, they actually forbid and deny it, because there is no category to "contain it."

To understand symbol, we must start with our first premise that the world is in process. Now make it a transitive verb, the world *be's* in process. Process is what the world is, not something that it does as an effect or a product. All process is "to other presencing." Symbol is the highest level of presencing, uniquely human self-initiating presencing in the image of God. Again symbol is the creative process of establishing transcendent permanent real presence of person to other.

Creation is *symbol*. Creation is not God creating a world full of things for others. Creation is *be's* God symbolizing himself, that is, God presencing himself to other. The creative presencing process in which the whole thing made is *be's* the presence of the maker. The gift is *be's* the real presence of the giver. The highest level of symbolic God-presencing is "*Word made flesh*."

"Word" is a symbol word. For us in our culture, "word," "logos," means the "tag" for the idea—or the idea for which it is the "tag," or the expression. This is where we are trapped in our *idea* culture. We put the truth in the idea and into correspondence to the reality of which it is the idea and proceed from there to the whole cultural answer to Pilate's question to Jesus, "What is the truth?" We fail because we say, "We have the truth," rather than saying, "We *are* the truth." As long as we say, "We have the truth," no matter what *truth* we have, we are never going to make it in the presence of God.

We must remember that for us the idea is a *product* of the person. It is not the person. By its own definition it is a reduction of the reality of which it is the idea and is true only to the point that it contains the "notes" of that reality. An *adequate* idea would contain all the notes of that reality and be *equal* to the reality of which it is the idea. Only God can have an adequate idea. (Please note that I am not inventing the idea that God has ideas; we have continued a trinitarian theology on that premise.) If I could have an adequate idea of tree, I could create a tree.

Our system has said in the human process of ideation the idea is a reduction of the reality of which it is the idea. It is further reduced when it is spoken of word because no word can contain or express all the truth of the idea of which it is the expression, except however in God.

Applying this to God, we come up with this adequate *idea* of himself. We will let this God be him to whom he gives infinitely adequate expression—the eternal *logos* or *word*—which eternal individual *substance* in divine nature is the second and distinct person who in time "became flesh and dwelt among us."

Now let us look at "Word of God made flesh." Person-presence—"Word of God"—means "Word that be's God." The Hebrew word "*dabar*" is not Greek "*logos*," which is the idea and/or its expression, but "*dabar*" means the person present speaking.

"Flesh" here means the total existential human reality. "Jesus who is the Word made Flesh"—is precisely by being *human*—by being the man that he is, is the total speaking presence of God.

It is time to recall the criteria of faith by which to judge all the affirmations made here. If what I say reduces the glory of God, the integrity or the glory of Christ the Risen One, or the dignity and freedom of human person, then reject what I have written. On the other hand, if what I say glorifies God, enhances the glory of the Christ and adds to the dignity and value of the human being and being human, believe it. This is so good, but never too good to be true.

In the creative process, God symbolizes himself, presencing himself to other. It is a *wording* or *speaking* process. As the Genesis text is rendered in English, it unavoidably takes on the categories of the language. There enters the inference of instrumental cause and effect; the word becomes the cause of the thing made. It is generally interpreted that God spoke the word, "Let there be," which word is the cause producing the effect which is the thing made. Then from this point, we proceed to explain all the works of God even into *church* and *sacrament* in categories of instrumental causality, e.g., argument from causality in the "*Quinque viae*," five ways for the existence of God.

The wording or speaking process, however, is symbolic. The word of God spoken is not the power that produces the thing, but it is the thing itself. As Jesus the man is "Word made flesh" by precisely being human, so it is through all creation. The tree is tree-word, the word made tree, the word made horse, etc., into *Word made flesh*. Creation is God speaking, symbolizing himself. Word made rock speaks God but it does not says it all, or even say as much as word made tree or word made horse, etc. When we arrive at "*Word made flesh*," God is in the process of saying it all when the process arrives at *image and likeness* in *Word made flesh* which is the human person. He is saying it all. God creating and God wording are the same God doing the same thing. God symbolizes himself. It is his final word because he says it all to the point that everything he wants to say and everything he has to say of himself, for himself, he is saying in us—the present moment of "Word made flesh."

Human experience in history is the revelation of God. (See the chapter "Revelation and Faith.") But it certainly hasn't all been said yet. In the process, in the creative wording, we are at the present moment of the Resurrection. Given the whole human condition—the human body that is the Christ—we have scarcely begun to see His glory. To summarize thus far, we can say: creation is the process that is God symbolizing or presencing himself. The Resurrection of Jesus is the present moment of creation; the church is the present moment of the Resurrection.

Symbol is not a substitute for reality; it is the ultimate reality of person present. Gifting, for example, is symbolizing—making the giver really present to the receiver. Any true gift is a gift of self. The gift is the real presence, sacrament of the giver. If I truly give a gift, the gift is (be's) me. The gift is not a substitute for the reality that is me. It is not to be received "as if" it were (condition contrary to fact) me, but it is me. If it is truly symbolic, it is real giving.

It takes mutual faith to symbolize. Here we come to the true meaning of the expression "to believe in" and "to believe into." Faith is the symbolic self-movement. We make things true by believing them. In the process of gifting, the giver believes himself or herself into the gift so that the gift really becomes the true presence of the giver. By authentically receiving, the "other" believes himself into the gift so that the gift is the real interpresence of the two persons, not one plus one but an *interpresence* which is love, friendship, etc. The gift is authentic not simply because it has been properly motivated, but because it is truly symbolic. It is the offer of real presence of (that is) the person who gives it to be entered into by the receiver.

Spoken word, written word, body language, touch, look, posture are all symbols in the subtlety and sensitivity to other awareness, insight and understanding that are involved in authentic symbolic communication. Symbolic communication is simply an authentically human interpresence. It is truly human cultural process.

Symbol is the process in which we *get in on* the experience of another as our own experience. At this point we must ban the word "vicarious" which is so commonly used. "Vicarious experience" is a reduction and denial of symbolic experience and presence. We reduce and deny sacramentality in the way we speak of Vicar of Christ. Vicar is a substitute for another, to be accepted "as if" it were the real thing. The Church does not "take the place of Christ," the Church by symbol is sacrament of the real presence of (that is) Christ. The Church is not a third party mediating the conflict between us and God. The good news is that there is no conflict. All is right with God. Jesus is in the *process* of being raised from the dead by the Father. Jesus is us and we are him. The symbol-sacrament process is that by believing we *get in on* his experience of dying *for others* (remember it must be for-other dying) and *get in on* his experience of being raised from the dead *for others* as our own experience. It is a real experience. We make it true by believing it. (See chapter on faith.)

To summarize the whole symbol-sacrament process: all of creation with Jesus at its head is sacrament that is real presence of God. Church is not an additional process, but it is simply the name and word we call the present moment of our involvement in the *cosmic process*.

The art of any culture epitomizes the symbolic process. The artist seeks symbolic-sacramental form for his or her experience. Consider the literary process as an example. Let us say that a friend and I have just returned from a harrowing experience of being lost at sea in a violent storm. We departed at dusk from port in good weather with everything ship-shape expecting an uneventful passage for our small two-person sailing craft. After passing the point of no return, we are overtaken by a sudden violent storm. Our mast is broken, our rudder lost. We are swamped aboard. My friend is heroic; he has his life on the line for me and does those things that puts his life at risk for me. I do the same for him. There is the terror of the howling wind, the darkness, the threatening waves, the wet, the cold, the helplessness, but by heroic effort and endurance, we survive and in the dying storm we are cast upon the beach.

Here we are telling the process not the story. When I return to my family and friends, what is the particular urgency? The urgency is to tell, *to word* my experience. Journalists will *tell about it*. When I tell you my experience, you get in on my experience, not *vicariously*, but you *get in on* my experience as your own experiences. You feel the terror, the cold, the dark, and also the heroic giving of self of my friend for me and I for him. I have given my experience symbolic form in the telling.

The *others* will *get in on* my experience in varying levels. Those with their own experience at sea will enter more deeply than those who have never been on the water. Because there are those who are better *hearers* than others, there are varying levels. Then there is the limit of my telling. Even at best, I am not capable of putting my total experience into words. There are all these limits in all symbolic communication.

Let's continue in the process. Now let us say that this is such a beautiful experience that it is suggested that I write it—not write about it. Thus "Passage to Remember" is written and published. It makes all the papers and even literary magazines and becomes a best seller. Everybody is reading and talking about it. It may be the best seller but not yet a classic; however, up to this point all who read it are getting in on my experience.

It happens that "Passage to Remember" lives on in multiple printings and is translated into the languages of the world. It becomes required reading for language courses and is ultimately established as a classic short story.

This has happened in the cultural process in the same way that all other art achieves classic status. A book or any other art becomes classic on merit. It not only somehow survives, but is accepted and installed and holds up as speaking for the people who are the culture. It not only speaks *to* them but *for* them. They read it and say "that's me," "that's us," "that's who we really are" or "would like to be." It is accepted on the merit that it speaks authentically for the people whose culture accepts it. It symbolizes them.

Classic Victorian literature, for example, speaks for the people of that age. It is the word, *image*, of what those people accepted, envisioned as what they wanted to be as human in that time and place. American literature proclaims the unique origin or quality or character that distinguishes our culture. Many books are written. Many have a passing day of glory, but only those that consistently and constantly speak for the people that are the culture become the classics.

The books of Holy Scripture have come about by the same process. There have been many writings both in Old and New Testament that were beautiful, inspiring and uplifting in their own time, but somehow didn't have the timeless quality that qualified them to speak for the people to all other people for all time. The Apocrypha are a collection of beautiful writings that didn't quite make it. The Scripture is simply the classic literature of the people of God. As every other classic proclaims the unique character of the people whose literature it is , the Bible proclaims that the people of God are a unique people born of faith in God and live by faith in God. They have come to the awareness that their origin from God is in the tomb of Jesus, whose unique character is the gospel life for others and whose destiny is their return to the Father in His vision of glory. The Bible is simply the classic literature of this people. It does not denigrate the Bible, it does not reduce its *inspiration* or in anyway deny its unique character or authenticity as Word of God to affirm that it came about in an authentic process. In fact, such is the ultimate establishment of the Holy Scripture as a living Word of God, who wants to be known as the God of the people who believe in him.

Let us return to the literary classics and to the process that is symbol. I have Shakespeare's *Hamlet* in hand. Do I read *Hamlet*? or do I read Shakespeare? Or is there really a difference? Yes, there is a difference. If I understand Shakespeare, I read Shakespeare. His writing is his real speaking presence to me. In my reading *Hamlet*, he and I enter into an intense interpresence as he give symbolic-sacramental form to the personal experience of infidelity, false promise, and the tragedy brought by ambivalence and indecision. The *book* is the author present speaking for those who can *read* him. His art, his drama is symbol, not just a record of what he did, but an immediate speaking presence. In his literary art, he achieved symbolic presence, permanent transcending real *living* presence of person.

We do not reduce or remove the Gospel according to John as the real speaking presence of God in Jesus by saying that this version of the Gospel is the symbol of the faith experience of the community that authored it. Rather, it is precisely because it is symbol of that faith that we *get in on* the experience in our own time and our own place, on their experience of hearing and believing in the man John, who hears the Christ, who hears the Father speaking. It is more intensely and more completely *word made flesh* in us who believe and speak this moment than it ever has been before. This process is not a series of diminishing returns, but an expanding presence.

By demand of our culture, much of what we call the "Bible" as a fixed and officially declared list of books—which is called the "Canon of Scripture"—is a closed entity that not only forbids any change or addition to the text, but even forecloses any new revelation. In the process of its becoming the literature of the people of God, there was by cultural promise and expectation a faith awareness that the presence of God was itself a revealing process and that the Scripture was allowed to grow with the people whose faith was its source and its authority. In our culture, we have to have categories so we say that there are two sources of faith: *Bible and Tradition*, written and spoken revelation. Here there are two *fallacies*. The first is that the Bible and Tradition are the sources of faith rather than faith is the source of the Bible and Tradition. The second fallacy is that any division of "Bible and Tradition" into two entities is a categorical contrivance. Bible and Tradition are simply two aspects of one totally integrated process of interpresence of the speaking God and the hearing, listening people. This specific phenomenon is simply the leading edge of the cosmic symbolic process of God *getting in on* the living being of his people and his people *getting in on* the living being of their God.

"Process theology" is a current buzz word and claim for credibility. The most rigid of our traditional scholastic theology was a process, indeed a very logical process, which has taken all its premises by process to their perfectly logical conclusions. But it certainly was not a process theology! A process theology must not only posit the premise of cosmic process, but must itself enter into the cosmic process of revelation. Note that we enter the process with a constant and deepening awareness of the presence that is God. There will be no talk *about* God. His word speaks eminently well. The word and the work of God are self-authenticating and speak for themselves. We hope to get in on his process, to proclaim God's word and work, and hope and pray that his word and work authenticate us in the process.

7
FAITH AND CULTURE

PORTRAIT OF A BELIEVER

THEOLOGY AS ANY OTHER SCIENCE is an organized body of knowledge about a human experience with a specific reality. Theology is about the human experience with the mystery that is God. The human experience with the mystery that is God is *faith*. The beginning of this experience, the awareness that there is something about us and our world that is bigger than we are, confronts us with mystery.

Faith is no more and no less than the living answer to the question, "Who am I?" That answer in the total human response is *faith*; it is religion in any and all of its myriad forms and expressions.

The total answer to the question "Who am I?" is not only what we may be pleased to call *religious faith*, it is the ultimate premise for all decisions, for establishing a human society and for all value judgments by individuals and groups. A general agreement on this answer by a group of people is what makes a culture—a culture is a body of people who have a general agreement on what it means to be human, on human origin and destiny, on human values and human purpose and how to achieve it. Cultural premises are inherited, practically a part of the genetic package and as such are simply gratuitously assumed, hardly ever examined or questioned, but accepted as the way of life. This is what makes it a culture.

Cultural premises and assumptions are the source of religious premises, or are simply assumed as religious premises.

They are premises of faith because they are the premises for the answer to the question "Who am I?" The cultural process is the environment for the process of revelation.

The cultural answer to the question "Who am I?" is the cultural image which identifies, distinguishes and characterizes a culture. History shows that generally there has been little tolerance in cultural confrontations and the more powerful have always tried to make others into their own image by imposing their culture by force, law or conviction on a lesser group.

In our Greco-Roman culture, we start with a premise of faith in the *issue*. Believers trap themselves when they let the "atheist" say "I don't believe in God." In facing the issue logically, he must take the responsibility of saying "I believe there is no God," while believers say, "I believe there is a God." The atheist can't prove his premise anymore than the believer can prove there is a God. The atheist is caught in his illogic of saying, "I believe there is nothing to believe." By saying "I believe" the atheist must stand as responsible for his premise as those who believe in God. "I believe there is no God" is a statement of belief, not a grant of immunity.

This certainly does not settle the God question but it must be established that every person ultimately starts with a premise of faith. Every person in the structure or unstructure of the decision process that is faith accepts and starts with a premise that cannot be proven: "*I believe.*" There is no choice about that. All choice begins with what one chooses to believe and this premise of faith is the ultimate premise of every decision that any person will ever make.

This is the initial confrontation and tension between freedom and the reality of something other. In the process (and this is revelation) we don't come to know who God is by knowing who God is and what God says to us, but we know who God is by knowing who we are and what this says to us about our God, whoever or whatever he is to us. Knowing who we are *is what he says to us.*

The Mediterranean Basin has been for centuries the stage for ongoing cultural confrontations. At the time of Christ, the Greek culture in its specific Roman version was dominant in the area which, in our own cultural history, was the whole world. Cultural confrontations were settled by military might and the *Pax Romana* was a cultural establishment imposed upon peoples and nations which Roman arrogance was pleased to call "barbarian."

In Palestine there was a pocket of deep resistance to the *Pax Romana* by a people of a broad Semitic culture with their own unique but confused sense of world mission. These were the Jews. The Jews were a relatively small nation, a people of Semitic cultural origin. "Jewishness" or Judaism is a religion, not a nationality or a basic culture. The Jews are those Semites who are fathered in the faith of Abraham in whom all the nations are called to faith in the God of Abraham. By their call and their mission, they are a people "set apart," not to be separated and removed from all other people, but to call all other people to faith in the God of their Father Abraham. The Jews had their own cultural differences with the Samaritans whom they considered illegitimate in their own cultural family. Jesus invited them to achieve their world mission by sharing their cultural inheritance and destiny of a privileged chosen people of God with all other nations and cultures. They would not risk sharing it for fear they would lose it in the sharing, and thus they rejected Christ and all those who believed in him.

The gospel invited the Jews and all nations and cultures to reassess their cultural-religious premises and to accept a new and transcending image of what it is to be human—image of God—not by being better than others and by jealously guarding and hoarding as their own what had been given to them, but by coming into possession of these gifts by bearing them to all other people of the world. The paradoxes of the gospel, such as giving to receive or dying to live, were particularly offensive to the logic of the culture.

The disciples of Jesus, in a propitious historic-cultural moment, got underway the greatest religious movement in all history at least as we know it. The gospel found a world without hope, without vision, with life without purpose, people without dignity and freedom. The gospel was the promise that the Spirit of God is the human spirit for those who dare to believe it. The most remarkable promise and character of this gospel is that it is amenable to and works in any culture, but it requires a radical conversion of the Spirit and the rejection of those cultural elements that contradict or deny the human image of God as revealed in Christ.

Historically, the movement succeeds in establishing some new religious premises but really touches very little of the root cultural premises.

For centuries we have believed this way, because it seemed to be the case that the early Christian missionaries converted the Greco-Roman world and those converts in their turn *converted* the nations that lived beyond the boundaries of the Roman Empire, which the Empire arrogantly tried to ignore out of existence as barbarian. These barbarians wouldn't be ignored but rather invaded and overwhelmed the Empire with its social political structures. However, the culture of the Empire and even its Latin language prevailed in strangely altered forms and versions. Other languages survived, but in the process the languages were converted to contain the cultural Greek ontological categories and the Greek sense of time as part of the language itself.

But the survival of the Greek culture in the conversion process meant the survival and dominance of the cultural premise of the Greek image of man. A good case could be made for the position that the nations were converted more by the promise of the Greek humanism than by the promise of the Christian Gospels. What we have called the Christian Church in history has been largely an attempted compromise of the gospel with the humanism of the Greek culture. A culture can compromise, but the gospel can't and when a compromise is attempted between the culture and the gospel, the culture will always prevail.

The gospel speaks of our human involvement with God and with each other as the "mystery of the Kingdom of Heaven." It does not try to explain or prove. It does not promise or attempt demonstration or proof, but says rather "Try it. You'll like it." Yet in our ecclesiology, we start with demonstration and proof on the assumed premise that we have no premise until we have proven it. When the Church uses the cultural criteria to establish and prove the validity of its own claims, it has surrendered to the culture and has implicitly denied mystery by attempting to demonstrate and prove it.

The culture is the environment for the Church. The living culture is the existential human situation in which the Church is the people who make the culture and keep it alive and moving. The role of the Church is to make a charismatic search for the real human needs within the culture and to present the vision of the Risen One as the promise of all human fulfillment. The prophetic role of the Church is not to be anti-culture, but to speak to the culture and to speak against that part of the culture which denies or contradicts the gospel vision and promise of totally authentic humanity.

In our history, we have measured the vision by criteria derived from cultural premises. We have denied the gospel image by submitting and subjecting it to cultural criteria for proof and approval and by measuring its validity by the categories of our own cultural creation. The Greek image of man is a far cry from the image of God presented ultimately in the Risen One. Yet the Greek image has not only prevailed in our culture, the Greek cultural image has become the actual official teaching of the Church. We have attempted to explain the whole mystery of God in the ontological categories of our cultural philosophy.

The fact is that our theology itself has gratuitously accepted these cultural premises for its own process. The most devastating gratuitous assumption is the unquestioned acceptance of the Greek image of man for our own anthropology, our Christology and our own moral and ascetical theology. The devastating result of all this is the assumed and contrived premise that the Christ had to be more than human to be the Christ and we all have to be more than human to be saved. We are the culture that bemoans the fact that we are *only human*, yet we presume to measure and define the mystery of faith and of God in the categories of our own *only human* creation.

We submit the Word, God, to measurement by our cultural version of the *truth* and we accept the truth that is God on the condition that God accept our definition of the truth, or on the assumption that, indeed, he has so accepted it.

In the scene before Pilate in John 19, where Jesus affirms that his mission is to give "testimony" to the truth and Pilate cynically asks "But what is the truth?" we have in Pilate not only an image, but the archetype and symbol of the ongoing confrontation in history between the Church and culture. Jesus did not answer Pilate's question. He had already given it in Chapter 14. "I am the way and the truth and the life." The teaching function of the Church in the ongoing confrontation is not to make doctrine and dogma, but to present the man Jesus and his way of life to those who honestly ask the question "What is the truth?" and are willing to accept him who is the Word at his Word for the answer.

This is the faith that is the real premise of Christian theology. The human experience of living the gospel way of life is the faith experience that is Christian. That will be the premise on which we will attempt to build a valid scientific theology. All faith is search, a search for self and search for God. Search for God and search for self are the same search. When we find God, we find ourselves in him; when we find ourselves, we find ourselves in God. This is the real human creative process—this is the Christ; this is the Church. The Church is that which is going on between God and those who are searching for him.

All of this is a real and valid human experience; in fact, it is not real and valid unless it is human. As a faith experience this starts with a vision rather than with an idea or with closed-in, fixed categories. It is a real vision image to be achieved rather than an abstract foregone rational conclusion which can't reach beyond the human state that created it.

Our first task and responsibility in the process of establishing a new theology is to indicate and demonstrate the fallacies and failings of the old or traditional theology and then to assume the *burden of proof* or credibility for the new premises proposed. The first failure of the old theology is the arrogant assumption of ontology, the assumption of the adequacy for the *universal* categories, that is, that these categories can and do account for all of reality, including God. If these categories are adequate, they are also mutually exclusive and in them the whole cosmos and human person is divided and separated by an irreconcilable conflict.

For example, what is substance is not accident, and vice versa, what is absolute is not relative; what is matter is not spirit and so forth. We will first address the categories of substance and accident and their implications.

Substance and accident are the underlying universal categories. The view of all reality within these categories is that substance is the underlying ultimate substratum of all being, that substance is where things logically and ontologically begin to be. The substance of the thing is invisible and immutable, something which makes the thing in question to be what it is and to be precisely this thing and not something else. In this view, the *truth* is in the substance of things and in the culture.

Even people without formal metaphysics will affirm truth and reality with the words *substantial* and *substantially*. If the truth is in the substance of things, then it is *immutable and unchanging*, and hence we have our cultural hang-ups on *immutability* as the ultimate quality of truth and even of God. Change can be only in the accidents of things and any change or even progress can be *only* accidental, again with a very pejorative *only*. The categories became the measure of the truth, a kind of a *first truth*, a privileged truth that is never questioned and a truth that is granted immunity from the responsibility to defend itself.

The culture suffers and our theology with it from this disease of the *hardening of the categories*. This disease is transmitted culturally and is seen even genetically; it is epidemic and ultimately incurable. It reaches this terminal state when the last category is closed and this last category is the *absolute*. When a person closes this category, the whole world, all reality and even God, is frozen eternally into a category of our own creation. People will say "God is my absolute," and think that such is the affirmation of ultimate faith and that to accept God as absolute is the ultimate worship. In effect, this simply expects that God is to be pleased and honored to be put into a category or box that we have created for him and over which we maintain control. This problem itself is symptomatic of the disease of the *hardening of the categories*.

Another pejorative epithet in the battle is *relativistic* or *only relative*, and a genius like Albert Einstein is condemned for holding that the God of the absolutist cannot explain the world of science nor can the world of science explain the God of the absolutist.

We are all well aware of radical changes that have taken place in the formation of what we call the modern mind. This didn't just happen randomly in the cosmic and cultural process. The formation of the modern mind came about in the historico-cultural process by the dynamic of cultural forces which were the influences and ultimate credibility of the theories and implicit attack on the traditional cultural premises by four unlikely prophets who, even to this day, are rejected and condemned by many for their *blasphemy*.

These four cultural prophets are Karl Marx, Sigmund Freud, Charles Darwin and Albert Einstein. In their own fields, each of these men demonstrated the limits of the *absolute*. They were all process thinkers starting from process premises.

Karl Marx held that, along with the industrial revolution, human society was passing from a striated, fixed class, bourgeois society to a proletariat classless society. This has really happened and is happening in history and in our own lives. Marx's observation and premise were correct. His error was to attribute the process to an *inexorable* law and to exclude the dynamic human freedom from the process.

Sigmund Freud de-absolutized the human personality and posited a personality process which was observable and in many ways even measurable, but most of all a process that can be entered, influenced and directed. We may not agree with all his explanations and conclusions, but modern psychology and all behavioral sciences are premised on his theories of personality process.

Charles Darwin observed a continuity of identity in life forms and process that could not be explained by the biology of absolutely fixed species that demanded a separate and discrete act of creation for the appearance of each new species. He called for an organic structure and process to explain the continuity, progress and development of life forms on earth. He said simply that no life form is frozen but that there is a law by which the *best gets better* in continuity without interruption with all of its past.

Albert Einstein is image and symbol of genius in our culture. I suppose those who understand him would say that he moved mathematics, even in the popular mind, from a complicated system of accumulating and arranging units to a process that starts where we are and enters infinity in the organic structure of the cosmos. He affirmed the contradiction of the classic absolute and opened our minds to the *to-other* realness of relativity.

These four men had one thing in common. They were all process thinkers. They all saw the limits of the absolutes and opened our minds and our world to process thinking. These men have formed the *modern mind*. They have furnished the common premises for all modern science and theology as a science must start where all the other sciences start—God's world is a process world.

Theology is not the science of God *as such* or of God *in himself*, but the science of the human experience of God which we are pleased to call *faith*. In the process, we do not know who we are and what our world is because we know who God is, but we know who God is only by knowing ourselves and our world. This is the process of revelation. Theology is within this process.

Process is our first premise. Process is not just an abstraction or an ordered and measured change for better or for worse, or even a word for "something going-on," or something that something else does. Process is what the world is, not what it does. Process is what person is; process is what God is. We will have found God when we have found ourselves in process. Faith is the self-movement which is entry into the process.

Process is energy; energy is process. It is never neutral or without direction. It is creative or annihilative. It is good or evil at work; it is creation out of chaos according to the direction it is given. The direction of process is always *to other*. The creation or chaos of the process is determined by the other to which it is directed and everything becomes more or less, better or worse, beautiful or ugly, something or nothing, somebody or nobody, according to the other to which it is directed. God is totally for other—totally other for all and all for other.

We must get process out of the categories of substance and accident where process can be *only accidental* and not touch the substance of things because process is change. We must come to a three dimensional universe in which we do not say the world is *in process*, but rather that the *world is process*; that process, not substance, is the ultimate substratum of all being where they ontologically and logically begin to be. Ours is a process universe where the cosmic process becomes cosmic human person who is image presence of God—hence *PROCESS-PERSON-PRESENCE.*

Cosmic process becomes human person who is capable of self-initiated presence to other. In the whole universe, everything is what it is in response of other. There is for everything but God the primacy of the *other* and God is God by being first for all other. It is really inane to speak of God *in himself, God as such* or of *his internal processes;* all that he is, is God for others. In fact, the deepest revelation of the Old Testament was achieved by a people "at the bottom of the pit" in degradation and captivity, who became aware that Yahweh-God is *totally other.* Very simply that means they became aware that God not only means everything to his people; but that they, his people, mean everything to God, totally other for all and totally all for other. This comes clear in Scripture which proclaims a God who wants to be known and named as the God of those who believe in him, known by whom he is other to. It starts with the God of Abraham through the patriarchs and prophets and arrives at the present moment of revelation of God who is *Abba*—Father of Our Lord Jesus Christ and raises him up in glory in us. Jesus who is the man totally for others being raised from the tomb in glory in us is the final stage in the process of person to presence revealing God totally other.

Our culture tells us that the ultimate reality is "God as such, in himself," and that in all created things the ultimate reality is the *in itself* or *as such* reality. We speak of *morality as such, truth as such, trees as such,* etc. These are all abstractions. Abstracting and abstraction are peculiar to our culture and have a validity in our culture that they have in no other culture (at least as known to me). Semites, who have not been hellenized, do not abstract. Take "morality" for example. It is itself an abstract word but it is the word we use for all moral "reality," another abstract word. There are no abstract words in the original language of Scripture. As a person of our culture, how long could one speak about anything without using an abstract word? We further compound the situation by our categories of objective and subjective, and qualify truth as *purely objective* and as *subjective*.

In morality, for another example, we have objective and subjective morality and we hope we can bring our subjective morality into line with that which is the purely and totally objective, morality as such. People concerned about human right and wrong will abstract about the morality of human decision and actions *in themselves* by the process of abstraction. In abstracting they will clear the stage of consciousness of everything but the matter under consideration, focus on that matter exclusively and make a judgment about the rightness or wrongness of the act so considered. When there is relativelyuniversal agreement in judgment about the morality of this particular and specific *moral object*, it will be canonized as a moral principle, a statement of *objective*, and ultimately, as a statement of *intrinsic* morality, those things that are right or wrong *in themselves* and underlie the whole moral structure. Let us remember that *morality as such* is as much an abstraction as *tree as such*. *Morality as such* and *tree as such* exist only in the mind of the *as sucher* and are totally subjective. Still at a level of agreement about these subjective judgments, we canonize them as the ultimate reality by calling that, which really is only a corporately subjective judgment about morality, objective morality. This is an egregious fallacy.

Our culture does this with just about everything and the ultimate victim of the *as suchers* next to *God as such* is *human person as such*. Before speaking of human person we must note some other fallacies and establish errors in our way of speaking. We start with the first and worst. Our cultural image of being human is so lacking in value and dignity that we have a common complaint that we are *only human*, with a pejorative *only* and use our humanity as an excuse for fault and failure. In fact, our cultural image is so poor that it was not good enough for Jesus to be *only human*. We have had to continue a categorical and substantial personal divinity in a *hypostatic union* in order to explain him and his works. Then, we have had to contrive the trinitarian process in *God as such* to have a proper source and origin for the divinity of Christ. These two contrivances have become the core of the structure of the "teachings" of the Church with the result that we have a condescending God who has *intervened* in history to rescue us even though we are *only human*, even at best in the *state of original* justice, only analogous in his image and likeness.

At this point, let us enter the process of learning that we are in God's image simply by being human, by being self-aware, by entering the self initiated process of question and search in an awareness of the mystery of "I AM." We are in the image of God because we have a self initiated "I AM." A human person is a self-initiated "I AM." "I AM" is both an affirmation and a question and this affirmation and question or search is the first and ultimate premise of all human decisions. The answer to the question "Who am I?" is faith. How this question is answered in interpersonal relationships is religion.

What it is and what it means to be human is also the premise of our theology. We have stated that theology is the science of the human experience with God—which is faith. We start where God starts with us. He makes us into his image, and the image in which God made us must be the image we have of ourselves.

In the history of religion from ancient times, we find that ancient idolatry was not simply making weird or grotesque, fearsome images of *imaged or imagined* gods, but the expression of human experience with a mysterious other. They answered the question "What would I look like?" or "Where would I live if I were that other?" and came up with their weird, grotesque, fearsome images and places. It would, at first, seem that the Greeks were coming closer to the truth when they cast their gods into beautiful human images, but in reality they were moving further from the truth and this apparent refinement became the ultimate failure to which idolatry was doomed from the beginning. It failed not because it made too little of the gods, but because it made too little of men and women. The mistake is, it had the process reversed. It moved in the wrong direction. It cast the gods in the images of man rather than casting man in the image of God.

At the historic moment of the failure and death of idolatry, the Christ appeared and this man is the revelation of who God is by being God's man, God's image, by being authentically human. The authentic humanity of the Christ is the first premise of Christian theology, not the "divinity of Christ." In fact, image of man is the first premise of any culture and it is precisely at this point that the Christian gospels meet, confront, invite and challenge, any and every culture by presenting the man Jesus and his way of life with the promise of happiness and joy here and now by accepting and pursuing the gospel way. "I am the Way, the Truth and the Life" is an invitation addressed to all cultures and all persons. The mission of the Church is to proclaim this man, Jesus, and his Father's promise that the Word will be made flesh in the life of any person and in any culture that has the courage to believe, to risk taking him who is the Word at his Word.

The mission of Christian theology is within the mission of any culture where the Church lives. The mission of her theology is to present and to make the Christian image acceptable and credible, by comparison to, in addition to, or even by contradiction and invalidation of the cultural image. The cultural image is where we all are. Where we all are is where we believe, and where we are is the promise of our theology.

In the first place, we must be aware that the cultural image of human person is always a gratuitous premise in any culture. It is no different in ours which means that our cultural premise is the American version of the image of the Greco-Roman culture. Here we have the strong anomaly; the Church speaks vehemently against consumerism and the pleasure dimension of our Western culture, while it not only gratuitously accepts the cultural image but canonizes the cultural image by making it the official teaching image of the Church. The Church teaches that the cultural anthropology holds that "man is a rational being composed of a material body and a spiritual soul." The Church has been satisfied that this definition has been Christianized by adding a qualification and a kind of disclaimer. In Christian theology, it has become man is a *creature* (qualification) composed of a material body and a spiritual soul made in the image and likeness of God (disclaimer). The qualification "creature" rather than "being" is presumed to bring God into the picture and it does. "Made in the likeness of God" is a disclaimer of the philosophical origin of the definition and becomes an affirmation of revealed human purpose and destiny. But the anthropology and working definition of human nature remain the same. Man is still "body and soul" composite cast in the fixed categories of matter and spirit. From this point, we proceed to compound the confusion by adding the categories, faculties, passions and emotions.

The Greek image is struck largely and consistently within the metaphysical universal categories of the culture. The cultural philosophy arrogantly presumes that its universal categories are adequate and can account for and explain all of reality. It must be remembered that, if these categories are adequate, they are also mutually exclusive. What is matter cannot be spirit and vice versa, what is substance cannot be accident and vice versa and so on and on. Everything somehow falls into and is contained in these categories and they apply to all reality, including God.

When it comes to man, the first question is matter or spirit. Quite obviously, what the Greeks call *body*—note that this is not what the Semites or the Scripture calls *body*—is matter, yet strangely enough, phenomena appear and things happen that rise above and cannot be explained within the causality of that category. These phenomena can be explained only within the category of spirit. Quite obviously, categories somehow apply to the human phenomenon, but our Greek cultural forbearers, assuming that their categories were adequate, presumed to define man as a being composed of a material body and a spirit-soul that is person by reason of being individual substance in rational nature, etc. Our Christian forbearers in this same cultural process and history claimed to have Christianized and baptized this Greek image by bringing God into it, by saying *creature* instead of *being* and by adding "*made into the image and likeness of God*," as a kind of disclaimer at the end.

Thus the Greek image makes a person a kind of a figure "8," with one foot in each category of matter and spirit and because matter and spirit are mutually exclusive, there is built-in irreconcilable conflict, a conflict of human personality and that human problem and human purpose is to survive the conflict with the spirit prevailing. There is also the implication that all matter is evil, or at least the source of evil, and the philosophy does not say that all spirit is good, but that spirit can be good. It is not an even contest; the advantage is on the side of evil as far as being *only human* is concerned. But God has to be good and just and he will provide spirit help from without or from above to those who ask. (More about this later.)

The Greeks themselves had trouble reconciling a bad body with a good soul. How does one handle the problem of human passion and emotion and feeling that can somehow touch or even enter into the rational process? The Stoics tried to solve this by suppressing the feelings, emotions and passions. The Platonists tried to ignore them out of existence. Neither system has really ever worked but people are still trying to make them work; in fact many Americans, males especially, are a strange combination of Platonist and Stoic, e.g., "Little boys don't cry."

Our Christian cultural history is filled with many variations on the body-soul and image. Our moral and ascetical theology has used all the variations as premises for the vast variety of systems or methods that have been proposed. But they all have been variations and modifications of the same basic image that to be human is to be body and soul so that basically they all have the same premise.

While the body-soul image of man and woman has placed severe limitations on our awareness of what it means to be human, there are two other devastating implications and conclusions drawn from the gratuitous assumptions of the Greek image. The first and the most devastating is the cultural, even theological assumption, of the primacy of the individual. The second is the denigration of the human image, by accepting that it is not good enough to be human. A culture and a Church in which there is a constant refrain, we are *only human* and you had better remember it, and above all, remember it is not good enough to be human to be saved, do not proclaim Word made flesh.

The cultural premise of the primacy of the individual is not only devastating in its implications and consequences, it is itself a contradiction of the scriptural image. The first thing about being human is that we are a corporate person. When cosmic awareness became human—that's where we began to be human—in the human creative process, it emerged from the best awareness that preceded it; that best awareness was the gregarious or herding instincts of animals, identification not only with, but identification *as the whole group or body*. At the dawn of human awareness, the first human affirmation of identity or search for identity was "*We are.*" or "*Who are we?*"—not "*I am*" or "*Who am I?*" Cultural anthropology certainly affirms *a sense of community* prevalent in primordial and primitive human history.

In fact, history will bear out a prevailing *sense of community* among ancient peoples. The development of a sense of integrity and value of the individual was not inconsistent with or in any way a threat to the sense of the corporate even though in our Greek categorical culture that has logically happened. Instead of a creative tension between the individual and corporate, we have a devastating conflict of rights between the individual and the corporate with the presumption in favor of the individual and the corporate having always to bear the burden of proof.

In the history of our cultures, Semite and Greek, until about the eighth century B.C., the presumption was always in favor of the corporate. At that time, independently but simultaneously, both cultures advanced in social awareness and began to come aware of the integrity, rights and value of the individual *vis a vis* the corporate, that the individual was not absorbed into anonymity in the corporate, but within the corporate, the bearer and trustee of the total corporate right and dignity. In the Greek culture, it was the origin and development of the body-soul image of individual *person* in his own possession of a *nature* held in common with all others—*individual substance in rational nature*. The Greek sin was to think that individual possession of rights was a fragmentation of the corporate into equal parts standing over against each other in an adversary posture and the *community* became only an abstraction and the individual became the primary existential human reality—this is U.S.A. today.

It was at the same time in the eighth century, that this began to happen not too far away across the Aegean Sea in the Semitic culture and specifically as evidenced in the Book of Ezekiel where we find the first mention of individual responsibility in all of Scripture. The young Jews of the first deportation to Babylon were complaining that it was not fair that their personal present suffering in bondage was a punishment inflicted on them for the sins of their fathers. Ezekiel did not deny the corporate dimension of sin and responsibility but added to it the dimension of individual responsibility and proceeds to proclaim individual reward and punishment for keeping and breaking the law.

From this point on in the Old Testament, fidelity to the law involved both individual and corporate observance. Second Isaiah proclaims Yahweh's love and compassion for his Son, the Suffering Servant. The Suffering Servant first named the "Beloved," is the whole people called upon to give themselves for all the nations of the world. As a people they more and more rejected the invitation and by doing so rejected favor above all other people. They failed to be the people, corporate person, son, that they were called to be. The servant became a remnant and even the remnant failed until in Luke 1 we have *Mary*, the individual who is All of Israel, whose faithfulness is the faithfulness of all the people, and her faith is from the Christ who is the Suffering Servant winning the favor for all by giving himself for all. He is not the agent or proxy or third party representative for all others, but he is all others. He is sacrament or symbol of all people. He is all others living, loving, dying and being raised in glory from the tomb. To explain this, we need the theology of the reality of symbol and sacrament which will follow later, but for our present purpose, we see the full dimension of the individual and the corporate in sacrament or symbol. Jesus is not an agent or a third party; he is sacrament, the real presence of all mankind to his Father.

The people had failed to become a people, a corporate body or person. We cannot or will not be saved unless we become a corporate body or person. The first thing about being human is that we are corporate. This is the primacy of the corporate. We cannot be saved as an aggregation or assembly of individuals, nor can we be saved solo without or outside of a human community. However, *every* individual person is sacrament of the whole body, *human person*. In each person, there resides total human dignity and freedom and each person must stand responsible for the freedom of the total corporate person. Human freedom, for example, is corporate and as long as one person is not free no one of us is entirely free. The primacy and integrity of the corporate does not threaten or diminish the individual, but the corporate is the origin, maintenance and support of the individual. Even biologically, the genetic origin of the individual is so corporate that it includes all prior human generations and even shares in the cosmic origin of the universe. The origin and organic structure of the universe certainly calls for the harmony of having a corporate person in charge.

The Christian tradition in our culture has presented the moral imperative that each person must save his or her soul. This moral imperative of the individual salvation has had a devastating effect. Religion has become an individual and private affair and the *Church* is simply a group of individuals with the same ideas about saving their souls. How often it is said, "I'll have to save my own soul, even if everybody else goes to hell." Salvation is a corporate process and if everybody else goes to hell, so will I. There are no *solos* in heaven.

Anthropologically, the corporate coming to the awareness of the integrity and value of the individual was, at its time in history and in culture, a giant leap forward in the awareness— a great achievement in the corporate human process. It certainly did not in itself set up a conflict of rights between the individual and corporate but simply deepened and enhanced the awareness of human dignity. In the case of that people favored at that cultural moment with the possession of and the responsibility for the proclamation of the Word of God, it was the beginning of the revelation that not only a people, but each individual *belonging* to the people was to come fully into the "Image" of God by becoming the "Word made flesh" in the Spirit of the Risen One. It is interesting to note that Adam and Eve are corporate names—Mr. and Mrs. Everybody.

Those called to be the people of God failed to become such a people precisely by failing to accept the responsibility implicit in the faith awareness they achieved in their captivity in Babylon. In Babylon, they saw all the gods of the world. They saw the gods of all the other captured peoples because the Babylonian policy was to have the captive nations bring their gods to Babylon, on the theory that the more gods they had the better it would be for them. Yahweh their God was not only the one true God, but the one only God. The Hebrews saw that the gods of the other people were not just false gods with false promises, but that they didn't even exist. They were total vanity and contradiction. And if the Jews had the knowledge of and faith in the one only God, it was their responsibility and mission to bring their God to all other people and all other people to their God. They could not succeed in bringing all nations into being one people. If they could not really become a people themselves, they refused to share the privilege and favor that was theirs with others. This was their failure. The gospel of Jesus demands universal mission and sharing all privilege and gift of God with all others. It was precisely because of this demand of the gospels that they rejected Christ.

All of this indicates the primacy and centrality of our first premise, what does it mean to be human? How do we answer the questions "Who am I?" and "Who are we?" Are we *only human* or are we, by being authentically and totally a human community, "Word of God made flesh" in the spirit of the Risen One? Is each person, by belonging to other, an authentic person? Our faith is an individual and corporate self-movement into a human community.

Our own American cultural answer to the question is that we are *only human*. Each person is only an individual unit, in an adversary relationship with every other individual unit and with a larger community, under constant threat to his other individual identity and rights.

Hence, the first premise of our theology is the premise of faith that to be human is to be "Image of God." The word *of* is here the epexegetical genitive which denotes and affirms not possession or ownership, but identity correctly rendered, "Image that is God." Our Greek heritage forbids us to accept or proclaim identity here because its categories and logic cannot handle or contain it. It cannot accept identity with God so it says, theologically and culturally, "image of God" means *only analogy* to God, something like God but vastly different—a remote but somehow recognizable likeness, "God's up there" and "We are down here." God is where we are by our being there.

Genesis proclaims human origin and human destiny. Genesis does not speak of the process, of the biological or historical phenomena. It proclaims simply that God *"breathed"* Adam. Breath, in this language, is life itself not a means of life. The breath or life with which God breathed Adam is not less than, only part of, or analogous to, the breath or spirit that is God who does the breathing or spiriting. Adam comes alive with the life of God, the life that *is God*. Adam—that's us—has this life of God by receiving it, but what he receives is *all of God* and by receiving it, he is always and in every way totally dependent. The Spirit that he received, he was to come to possess by giving it back to God—to give it back to God by giving it to others. Old Adam refused and still refuses to give the Spirit and that is sin. New Adam is the Christ, born of the Spirit, and we are saved in him who has given his Spirit back to God and comes into the possession of the Spirit by giving it to others. "He gave up his Spirit" for others and now the Spirit is his to give to us. In receiving his Spirit *we are the Christ, we are him*, the image of God. That he is in us is what it means to be human. This is a premise not a conclusion, even though it has taken sometime and some length to present it. A rational philosophy must start with rational discovery; a faith theology starts with the faith vision of the Risen One.

Hence we do not say *man is a creature composed of material body and spiritual soul created in the image of God*, but rather we say, to be truly human is to be constantly and totally dependent, and to come into the possession of that spirit being given by giving it to others.

8
SCRIPTURAL CONTEXT

REAL PEOPLE IN A REAL WORLD

SCRIPTURE CANNOT BE REDUCED SIMPLY to a category of information or to such a thing as an academic subject matter. If we were to exclude all the other questions about Scripture, and ask "What does Scripture say about man's God?" or "What does it say about God's man?" we would always have the right questions. In making our search into Scripture, we must likewise be constantly aware that Scripture is written by believers for believers, and any and all search into Scripture is a faith search. The faith premise about God in the search is not that God exists, that there is God. The faith premise about God is a speaking God for whom being God is to speak and tell who he is. The Old Testament is constant in drawing the contrast between a "speaking God" and "dumb idols" who do not speak. In the ongoing process, there is the constantly deepening awareness that the speaking God is not only a caring and compassionate God that we can depend on, but that he is a fathering God to whom we can appeal in comfort and familiarity in whose Spirit "we cry *Abba*, Father." God has never withheld anything. To be God is to give everything and to say everything. To create is to reveal himself and to reveal himself is to create. Creation is speaking; his speaking is creation. God did not create and then wait countless ages to begin to reveal himself to Abraham. Rather, in Our Father Abraham, God finally found a believer, the first believer in our tradition. To return to the first question, "Do we know who we are by knowing who God is?" or "Do we know who God is by knowing who we are?" We cannot have a part of each for our answer. We must accept one of the questions to the complete exclusion of the other. The right question is now an affirmation, "We know who God is by knowing who we are." God wills to be known as the God of the people who believe in him and our faith is the answer to the question "Who are we?"

In speaking of cultures, we pointed out that the primary cultural premise that identifies and distinguishes culture from culture is the cultural image of man. How does the culture answer the question "Who are we?" "What does it mean to be human?" Whether it is called such or not, every culture has a religious premise. In our time in our own culture, we have made great discoveries into the mystery of the universe and great discoveries in the behavioral sciences, particularly into the mystery of human being and of being human. These discoveries are revelation. We have much more to believe and more to believe in, in the ongoing creation-revelation process. But it is a process of knowing "who God is by knowing who we are." We affirm God and come better to know him by affirming authentic humanity, but we deny God by rejecting and denying authentic humanity. This is "sin."

This is the human process and it is precisely within this process that the Christ appears. He is "Word made flesh." Word of God means word who is God. "Word" means speaking presence of person. "Flesh" means "total existential human condition." It affirms "this man Jesus is the total speaking presence of God." He is God speaking precisely by being totally authentically human. He is the ultimate human achievement, the man born of faith who is himself the ultimate believer who went to death believing his Father, *Abba*, would raise him up. He has achieved "image of God."

The Christ is all and everything that it means to be human. It is by the living experience of being the Christ that we know all that it means to be human. We must again return to basic premises. The world is process. The world is the process of God being other to the world and world being other to God. This creative process is presencing or symbolizing; it is sacramenting. Whatever God's name is, it must be a *verb*. Our name also should be a *verb*, an action word. "Sacrament" also must become an action word in which we could say it all by saying, "Jesus is Sacrament" of (that is) God and we are Sacrament of (that is) Jesus. God and his world are not two presences, somehow juxtaposed or placed side by side, but God and his world are interpresence, sacrament and symbol, in which creation is the permanent establishment of the transcending person-presence that is God.

There is ineffable mystery here, a mystery that cannot be spoken in token words, but only in "Word made flesh." It is the mystery of human spirit and human freedom. In the mystery of "Word made flesh," which we are with the constant divine initiative, we are constantly being created. Word is not made flesh until there is the free self-initiated response by which we enter and achieve sacramental union. Our human response to God is our response to other human person. Simply stated, "What we are to others, we are to God." By being totally the man for others, Jesus is the presence of (that is) God to us. This man gives us our name, our identity. He is (be's) us and we (be) him.

In this matter, we who call ourselves Christian have a traumatic identity crisis. On the surface, it would appear to be a case of multiple personalities, a kind of schizophrenia or a manic depressive movement between stages of delusion of grandeur and hopeless depression. Really, it is nothing more than a Babel of confusion brought on by our own ignorance. It started with Adam whose sin was to presume to tell God who he was, rather than to let God tell him. Our confusion is of the same kind. We have such confidence in our own devices and systems and in our own logic, that we presume to tell God how to speak and what to say. We look for the magic formula and end up in a big fight in which everybody is saying "my formula is better than yours" and we have a confusion of tongues rather than a pentecost in which "we all hear them preaching in our own language."

We might borrow an expression and intend no pun when we say the correct language is "body language." The language that is people being people to people and, by being people to people, being and becoming people to God. This is being and becoming the body that is human, but it is the body that is Christ. Remember that in Scripture the word *body* means person present *to other*.

We cannot improve on God's way of saying it. He says it in "Word made flesh." We say it simply by being and becoming "Word made flesh." The Gospel way of life is the only adequate and valid proclamation of "Word made flesh" and the only correct answer to the question, "What do you think of the Christ? Whose Son is he?"

Our problem is not only the inadequacy and error of any and all of the attempts at doctrinal formulations, it is a reduction and denial of human dignity and the integrity of human freedom, and a refusal to believe and to accept the real glory of being human. We presume to measure "God's Holy One" by the limited criteria set by our own very inadequate cultural image and keep on insisting that God be the God we think he should be, and that the glory of the Christ that is revealed in us is too good to be true.

The radical error here is the failure and refusal to accept the immediate symbolic and sacramental presence of God. We insist that God is up there, operative from a distance through various systems and series of instrumental causality. This is the premise that demands that "Christ" be from "out there" sent by God to intervene *on our behalf* to do that which we could not do for ourselves because we are *only human*. The conclusion or result is not only the affirmation of *more than human* in the categorical substantial *Divinity of Christ*, but also the implication of a *third party*, a *somebody else*, a *somebody other than we are* who somehow *volunteered* and *took up our cause*. Certainly, there are elements of this that are very true, but the implied assertion that Jesus is the *third party* from the outside who has taken up our cause is devastating.

Our attempts at formulation of the *right doctrine* have established a structure with God *up there* and us *down here*. There is also the presumption of conflict between us and God being mediated by Christ at his historical moment and now being mediated by his Church which he has left here to take his place, because he has returned to his Father *up there*.

This is fraught with error upon error. First of all, *God is love*, and all of his self-revelation to us in our sin is an invitation to return to love. I suppose it is not surprising that the disobedient child thinks that the Father is angry. As to conflict, the good news is that all is right with God. The Church, as a third party, is not here to mediate our ongoing conflict with God, but the Church is our established interpresence with God in the *Resurrection of the body* that we are, the *body* that is Christ, and the Church is the sacramental process in which we are raised up in glory in the presence of the Father.

We have recently come through a phase in theology which was an attempt at sophistication by distinction and separation. This was the treatise by many theologians some twenty years ago to return to the *historical Christ*. This was an attempt at realism, that it was necessary to return to the *historical Christ* to re-learn who he really was, to return to a real gospel faith in Jesus Christ. The fact is that the only real Christ is the Christ being raised up in us, the continuing sacramental moment that is the Church. It is true that discoveries in history and archaeology and in cultural origins give some new dimension to understanding the gospels that is the affirmation of an historical moment, but the speaking and the listening of the Word made flesh is always the present moment. The Christ is how and when, and where God is present to us and us to God. The Christ is what and who we are to God and God to us in the urgency and immediacy of sacramental inter-presence. There is nothing *past* or *gone by*. It is all here right now forever.

Another cause of trouble is the unavoidable confusion that arises from any attempt to put Hebrew thought into Greek words. Given the cultural reality, Greek words cannot be used without somehow accepting the categories that the word expresses in their cultural context. The problem here is the word *mediator*. The Hebrew, Paul, thought Hebrew, but wrote and talked Greek and speaks of Jesus as "mediator between God and man." The author of the Letter to the Hebrews was a Hebrew who thought Hebrew, but talked Greek and speaks of Jesus as the "Mediator of the New Covenant."

Our word *mediator* in English is the Latin rendering of the Greek word which really means the same thing. The Greek and Latin root is their word for *middle*, out of which we get *middleman, in between, go-between,* and so forth. Add to that our cultural fixation and compulsion to explain everything in the categories of causality, and the go-between, middle-man, becomes an instrumental cause and even God is spoken of as ultimate and uncaused cause. Jesus the Mediator inevitably becomes the third party-go-between, and our sacramental theology becomes an exercise in all the categories of causality.

From this, we have proceeded very logically to a complex structure and series of intermediaries and intercessors between us and God. We have made the ascension of Jesus a return to the Father *up there* with a *glorified* humanity to become our intercessor. He has left the Church here *to take his place* as a kind of substitute presence. His return to the Father is not that he leaves us, but his return to his origin—the self movement of His total faith in which he has given himself back to God in his total giving to others. As God wants to be known and to be the God of those who believe in him, and his glory is his people, likewise, the ascension of this son is his being raised up in glory in the vision of the faith, that this is what it means to be totally authentically human, and that this glory is not what he somehow is to us as another person, but that this is who we are in the presence of God.

The ascension of Jesus is a continuing process. The question remains, "What do you think of the Christ?" The process is the same process by which we venerate Mary and honor the saints. We are not denying the dimension of *for us*, because *for other* is what it is all about. *For us* is who he is, and who and what he is *for us* is who and what he is to God. It is all going on right here in an urgent, immediate inter-presence. *Immediate* means with no medium, or go-between, or intermediate cause.

In our structure and series of mediators, we have not placed Mary next to Christ, but below him, but still we have insisted that she is Mediatrix of All Graces. It is really a complex system. We have insisted that all our prayer and petition come through Mary, to Christ, to God, and in return flow grace and favor from God through Christ, through Mary to us. Then there are the saints below Mary, but somehow established in a hierarchial order from the lowest to the highest place in heaven which again becomes an order of influence to the throne of God which can be approached only through proper channels, controlled by proper authority.

The first fallacy of this contrived structure is the gratuitous assumption of the necessity of intermediary and of instrumental cause, that Jesus and the Church and the saints are a third party agent between us and God. Whereas we are the Christ and being the body who is Christ, we are the Church, and being the Christ and the Church means that we are in the immediate presence; church is us in interpresence with God.

A second fallacy is in the implication that follows from our very poor cultural image of being only human. It is the implication that we really are not very good at praying, and that it would be arrogant to presume that our prayer is worthy and fully pleasing to God. There is the implication that at very best our prayers are flawed and need to be improved by having somebody proven better than we are offer them in his or her name on our behalf. This includes nostalgic references to the "age of saints " and the "age of miracles" as the "good old days" and a nostalgic desire to have been present "in the days of Jesus," or such questions as "What would Jesus do if he were here?" "If he were here" is a statement of condition contrary to fact, an affirmation that he really isn't here. Whereas he is our real presence to God. We celebrate Christmas with the implication that the Infant of Bethlehem is Jesus at his best. It's too bad he had to grow up. The present moment of faith is always Jesus at his best. I can remember being required in high school history to read Walsh's *The Thirteenth, the Greatest of Centuries*. If the thirteenth was the greatest of the centuries, every century since then has been a failure.

In all of this, we have another classic instance of beautiful faith, but very poor theology. The process remains that our God is a God of people, that he wants to be known and glorified as the God of the people who believe in him. At the risk of hearing violent charges of impiety and even blasphemy, I will state that the function and duty of religious people is to make something of God by being his people.

The faith of the people of God is the creative process and the creative presence. As far as true religion is concerned, the issue is not, "What do we make of God; how great do we make him?" How great God is in himself and how easily he could get along without us is a completely inane speculation. In the process in our faith, we ascend (transitive verb) the Christ; we raise him up in glory in our faith. We likewise "ascend" Mary, the woman of faith, in whom God has found favor in us and in whom we find favor with God. Then there is the host of God's holy ones in whom God has been constantly glorified, whom we also raise up to glory. Faith deals with images and living presence and makes God true to his people and the people true to God. This is the creative process, for truth and holiness, in which the word and the work of God are self-validating. God's word and work are validated by people believing in them, not by "infallible" statement and declaration of sanctity by official proclamation through proper channels. Ascension of Jesus, Assumption of Mary, Canonization of Saints is all very real. It is the work of the faith of the people, not the result of official declaration by an ecclesiastical process or authority, but in the ascension process of faith and the affirmation and celebration that we are a holy people. An interesting note is that to preserve the "divinity" of Jesus it has been and is still being said that he "raised Himself" from the tomb and "ascended" to heaven by "his own power." Hence, these verbs have been kept in the active voice. Mary was not divine, so for her we have used the passive voice, Assumption, "was assumed," "was taken," etc. We have preserved the "divinity" of Jesus by saying he worked miracles by his own power and "raising himself" from the dead was the ultimate miracle. We should use the passive voice for Jesus, too. He did not raise himself from the dead. He is being raised up in us who are his body. He is who we are and we are who he is. Of Mary and the saints, we have said, God works miracles "through them." This is the evidence of our overriding premise of God working through intermediated cause and the theological compulsion and scruple to keep Mary and the Saints "only human." If Mary or St. Paphnutius are involved in a real miracle, we do no dishonor to God nor do we arrogate undue privilege or power to Mary or Paphnutius if we say Mary or Paphnutius worked the miracle. We don't have to say God worked the miracle through them. In fact, that is the way to give proper honor to God. That is the way God would want us to say it. The best way to give due credit to God is to say the saints worked the miracle.

We return again to the strange and violent things we have done to the gospels because of our cultural premises and consequent theological scruples. By reducing the miracles to a category of exceptional works which prove Jesus is the great exception to the rule and limitations of being "only human" because he was substantially divine, we misread and abuse the real work that they are and deny the real credit that they deserve. No miracle in the gospel is offered as a "proof" of anything. Every miracle is a spoken promise and every miracle is a work of human compassion. Jesus says to the beneficiary of the miracle, "Your faith has made you well." He never says, "I worked this miracle to reward your faith." Likewise the gospel says, "He had compassion....He took pity" and this does not say that when he "had compassion" or "took pity" that he called on a reserve source or divine power and worked the miracle, but rather is it always a clear affirmation that the miracles were the work of his human compassion and pity, and they are the promise that those who believe in the "Word made flesh" will, by believing, become the word made flesh themselves and, by their pity and compassion, perform the same miracles and will perform even greater works. Real believers in the Word of God by their faith become the real living loving presence of God, doing the wondrous works of God by their immediate sacramental presence, not as a remote link in a chain of causality.

In our Roman Catholic tradition, we have a beautiful faith and constant awareness of "real presence" and sacrament. Our faith in real presence and sacrament has been constant and beautiful; our theology has been constantly atrocious. We must return to our origin with the courage to take him who is the Word at his word. It is beautifully stated in the Gospel according to Matthew. In Matthew's infancy narrative, he cites Isaiah 7/14 and says that the promise is fulfilled. The promise is not that there will be a "virgin birth," but that the child born will be "Emmanuel." The word is "Emmanu-el" rendered "God-with us-is." This is not just an affirmation of fact that God is somehow present, a fact about God. It is, rather, the name of the people, the name of those who believe in him. In this language and culture, to name is to give identity. Name is "person-word."

Naming is a promise to be believed, the making of the person. This child who we are is "God with us," not the name of God, but the name of the people of God. The gospel closes with the affirmation of the promise fulfilled but the affirmation and promise is lost in the translation into our languages. There is an inconsistency in that the same name-word is rendered differently in the last verse of the gospel than it is in the infancy narrative. In the rendering of Matthew 20/20, the name "Emmanuel" becomes a phrase, a promise with a kind of future orientation, traditionally interpreted as a promise that Jesus will remain as an abiding guiding presence. "And behold, I am with you all days, even to the end of the world." It would seem that when the name is used in the beginning as an introduction to the whole work, that when it is recalled at the end, it would be used in the same way with the same meaning. Thus "Emmanuel" in Matthew 20/20 would be a name and a naming, a promise fulfilled, the second book-end enclosing the whole good-news proclamation, an affirmation of promise fulfilled in the believing "Remember Emmanu-el all days until the end of time." It is the naming of the believers, Emmanuel, now that's you, *your* name is "*God with us.*" Live up to the name and keep the promise. It is not a name of God, but a name of the people of God. It is not a promise that God *will* keep; he has kept his. It is a promise that we must keep, that our name is "*presence of God.*"

Our name is "God is with us" in an immediate inter-presence. Our distant God "up there" accessible only by a third party intermediary is not even as good as the "primitive" awareness of the people of the Exodus for whom, according the tradition of origin, the saving presence of God is in the image of the cloud or the pillar of fire. Both are the image of an immediate presence that penetrates, but does not consume. This is in contrast with the image of the inaccessible idols, who forbid access or approach, and to enter their presence as instant annihilation.

In the process of our faith, we ask the question, "How great is it to be human?" True faith is the search for true human identity, and the religious process is ultimately to become perfectly human person. Paul speaks of the process in his Letter to the Ephesians, "to knit God's holy people together for the work of service to build up the Body (person) of Christ until we all reach unity in faith and knowledge of the son of God and form the perfect human person, fully mature with the fullness of Christ himself." (Ephesians 4/12-13.) This is the process that is the Church.

In the Church-process we ascend (transitive verb). We raise him-ourselves up in glory in our faith. Our faith is our awareness of who, what and where we are to God, right here, right now in a continuing moment. It is an awareness of urgency. "God with us" is constant total giving, and all that we are and all that we can be is response to presence that is God. That response of self-awareness "me to God-God to me" is faith and when we name and articulate this response, we pray. Faith is the search for self and search for God. Prayer is faith at work. Search for self and search for god are the same search. When we find ourselves, we find ourselves in God and when we find God, we find ourselves.

The common question about the intercession of Mary or the saints or directing our prayers to Mary or the saints is a wrong question and whatever answer is given will simply further confuse the issue, which should be no issue at all. The question starts in the wrong place and is asked from the assumed premise that we are at a distance from God and somehow the gap must be bridged.

It all starts with making Christ a third person and intermediary between us and God. Our doctrine and dogma will affirm identity with Christ, that the Church is the body of Christ, that we are the Christ etc. Doctrine and dogma notwithstanding, that is not the way the Church prays "officially." Officially we pray "through Christ our Lord" and "through Mary and the

Saints." In fact, all of this is compounded by making the Church a third party that does our praying for us. While it is true that the original use of the formula, "through Christ our Lord," did not imply any third party intermediary nor did the title "Lord" imply or affirm divinity but as understood and used today, it has both these implications. In fact, great effort is put forth to bring about a Liturgical Renewal to teach us and to learn better how to pray to Christ to pray to God for us. Rather, the renewal that is needed is to come to the faith awareness that we are the Christ praying to the Father in our own right, in *our own* name with the glory, dignity and status of most favored son-daughter. When we become aware that we are the Christ praying to our Father, Mary and the saints come into proper perspective. Mary and the saints are simply who we are. Of course, there is glory and praise. Of course, there are wondrous works. Of course, there are gloriously heroic lives deserving of acclamation and proclamation. But they are us, and we do not come to God through them, or somehow ask them to be our agents, intercessors, or advocates. They are us and we are them, and we who pray enter the presence of God with the confidence and sense of worth and dignity that we belong, that we are comfortable and at home with our Father "in heaven." Heaven is where we all, saints and forgiven sinners, are at home with God and God with us.

9
RESURRECTION

THE GLORY OF BEING HUMAN

THE RESURRECTION IS NOT A TEACHING or a historical fact, but a primary living cosmic reality. If we were to make a list of the most misunderstood or least understood "teachings" of the Church, at the top of the lists would be the most important, the most central teaching of all—the resurrection of Jesus Christ. In fact, it is downgraded and misrepresented even by being called a "teaching" or a doctrine. Calling the resurrection a teaching is like calling "We are human" or "We are American" a teaching. What it means to be human, to be people or what it means to be American need specification and explanation as we go along. In the same way, we would not say "We are Christian" is a teaching of the Church. Being Christian means that we are the Resurrection People.

To say that being an American is the most important thing about being people is wrong. To say that being an American means that we are not Mexican, or Canadian, or British, would likewise be inadequate and ultimately wrong. In our religious identification, we have even greater confusion. For the most part, we make "I am a Christian" mean "I am not a Jew, or a Moslem or a Hindu, etc." Then we come to the most confusing question, "What kind of Christian are you?" Our answer, "I am a Catholic, and a Lutheran and a Baptist, etc., becomes illogical, confusing and unchristian. To save the situation we ask, "If you all call yourselves Christian, what do you have in common?" The answer is most likely to be a cliche or a platitude something like, "We all believe in Jesus Christ." In an attempt to be more sophisticated, we might respond, "We all believe in the divinity of Christ." When we begin to hear the explanations for these questions we have Babel revisited—and like the Biblical Babel, the worst thing is that the people don't know that it is Babel. Those who recognize the new Babel don't try to sort out and unconfuse the Babel; they pray for a new Pentecost—a new hearing of the message. The message is "good news"—"He is risen; He is alive."

In order to have a new Pentecost, we do not need a new message. There is still news and it is still "good news" or god-spel—gospel. But to have a new Pentecost, we need a new hearing, more questions and even some new questions. Our first problem is that we have let the good news become old and it is no longer news. While we may believe that Jesus rose from the tomb, we have re-buried him in our Greek cultural sense of time and have come to accept the resurrection primarily and exclusively as a demonstrable historical fact. From that point on, we have called the acceptance of the historical fact, faith in the resurrection.

To return to our previous questions about identity, let us take a Christian and a Hindu. Our Hindu friend is an honest man seeking the truth and comes to the typical Christian for information about Christianity. The typical Christian very properly starts with the call of Abraham; takes his Hindu friend through the Old Testament history of the people of God, into the historical Christ event. By the argument of prescription, he reasonably demonstrates that the resurrection of Jesus is a historical fact, that it actually happened. At that point, the typical Christian will say, "There it is; it is proven. Jesus really rose from the dead. I have made my case. Christianity is the true religion." The Hindu will say at this point, "That's all very well. His resurrection, as an historical fact, must have been wonderful for him and for his friends. What is it to me?" Our Hindu friend would not be unduly cynical by adding, "So he rose from the dead—so what? What do I get out of believing that?" We won't let our typical Christian continue and say, "If you believe that, that makes you a Christian."

Rather let our typical Christian say, "I see your point. I'll have to ask a few more questions myself." Let's proceed with the question and return to the message. The message stands "He is risen." We must keep the message in present tense and hear it for the on-going present proclamation that it really is. We must also become aware that if he has died for us, he is risen for us. And if he is risen for us, where is he now? and how is he there? Our typical Christian has had typical answers for that one. Some have said he is "in heaven" at the "right hand of the Father," but he has left the Church here "to take his place." Others have said he is really transubstantially present, body and blood, soul and divinity under the species of bread and wine in the eucharist. Others have said the Church is "like" a body and he is present in us "as if" we were his real body.

The faith of each answer is real and is right, but the theology is atrocious. It is true that he is at the "right hand" of the Father, but that is right here where we are. "Right hand" is a statement of status, of acceptance and exultation for his achievement. He hasn't left the Church as a substitute presence to "take his place." The church is his on-going real personal presence at the right hand of the Father. He doesn't have to go "up there" to be with his Father, because his Father is here where we believe in him. The eucharist is his real full resurrection presence, but the eucharist is people, not ritual. The eucharist is people being the Risen One, people being people to people, believing people in his Spirit, being the real living body-person that is the Christ that the Church is.

At this point, we don't want to give the impression or the promise that we are proving anything or that there is anything to prove. We can prove only those things that are smaller than we are. We won't insult or deny this mystery by attempting or promising to prove it. We come to our most authentic and most real possession of the truth by believing, not by proving, and it is only by believing that we find joy and consolation and confidence in the truth that is our God. This bit of theology is important here because it is precisely by our faith in the Risen One that we come to our God and that our God comes to us.

Let us return to the questions to be asked. We have asked and somehow answered, "If he is risen and alive, where is he? How is he where he is?" We have made affirmations about his real presence in the Church and in the eucharist, etc. If Mary, the real believer, was permitted to ask, "How can this be?" I am confident that the same question is permitted to us. We will have to accept the same answer. It is the work of the Holy Spirit and the power of the Most High.

We are, however, not faulting faith or doubting the Word if we make a search and ask questions to become more aware of our presence to the Father in the Risen One and enter more deeply into the mystery. It is not a mystery of darkness but a mystery of light. It is not a mystery hidden and forbidden, but a mystery revealed and open to the discovery that the resurrection of Jesus is what we are. It is our presence in the glory of the Father, the ultimate revelation that we are good enough for God.

In our own time and in our own way, we are involved in the same faith search that Jesus experienced on his way to death and resurrection. Jesus had a problem about his mission—not that he was unwilling to carry out his mission—but there seemed to be confusion and even contradiction in what he was expected to do. At his birth and at his baptism by John, he was proclaimed to be "son of God, most favored." This was the name and title of the Suffering Servant whose total faithfulness would bring him to die for others. On the other hand, there was "Messiah," the Anointed One, the "CHRIST," the fulfillment of promise, achievement of glory, before God and all nations. The problem was how could these apparent contradictions be reconciled? How can one person be both Suffering Servant and Messiah?

The transfiguration is the experience of joy in finding the answer to the troubling question. Suffering Servant and Messiah—suffering and glory—are not mutually exclusive. They are not contradictory. They are not only compatible, but complementary and belong together not by some strange contrivance but in the wisdom of God's ways. It is simply the only and best way to come to glory. Sin hasn't changed the plan of creation, but given the dimension of sin, the glory achieved in the plan is even greater.

There is no way to come to resurrection except through the experience of death. Faith unto death and into death is entrance to our resurrection. Again, the resurrection is not merely historical fact but the reality of the present achievement of faith. There is the anguish and even the uncertainty of the search and the transfiguration joy of the vision and the certainty of the answer. Jesus approaches his death, the Suffering Servant transfigured in faith, and rises out of death transformed in glory. In our own faith experience, promise of resurrection is real and it is at hand. It is proffered as a gift, yet the resurrection is the achievement of the faith of each believer as it is the achievement of the faith of Jesus. In the church-sacrament process, we get in on the Christ experience of search and discovery and final achievement as our very own personal experience. The Suffering Servant is not unnamed. The Suffering Servant becomes the Messiah. "How can this be?" It is by the power of the Most High.

Before we attempt theological explanation of symbolic process and sacrament of how the death, resurrection and ascension of Jesus is going on in us which is the Church, we will first reassess the reality of resurrection. What happens in resurrection is what happens to Jesus in death, resurrection, ascension, because that is what is happening to us who believe ourselves into the Risen One.

In the first place, death-resurrection-ascension is one entity, a simultaneous happening. His death is his resurrection, is his ascension. The three dimensions of this simultaneous, all at once happening, of necessity are revealed to us sequentially and seem to be a series of three discrete events following one another. It had to be revealed in this way because of the nature and the limitations of the human situation in which and to which it was being revealed. We couldn't have taken it all at once.

Futhermore, the situation was such and remains such that it has to be demonstrated that his death is real. He really dies. We have to be taken where we are, where we think of death and what we think death is. Jesus and those who believe in him can be open to no charge that this death was a fake and the claim of resurrection a hoax. In the larger historical situation, it must be established by credible witness that the death of Jesus is a real historical fact. He really did die.

This first credible witness to the reality of His death is simple and convincing. His friends buried him. Beyond that, he was executed under Roman criminal law and his death was properly and dutifully certified and reported to proper authority as ordered and required by the law. Even those who, at the time, denied the resurrection could not charge that he didn't really die. They accused his disciples of removing his body and burying it in a different place. And so today and for all time, no one can reasonably raise the objection that he didn't really die.

His death is real but what is it really? What happens when he or any other person has the experience that we call death. At the grave of his friend Lazarus, Jesus told the grieving Martha, "I am the resurrection and the life. Anyone who lives and believes in me really never dies." John 11/25. He does not say the experience and appearance of passing is not real, that there is no cause to grieve, that grieving and sorrow are inane and foolish. What he does say is that what we have seen and experienced is really not death.

If we ourselves had been on Calvary at the foot of the cross and had had the vision to see what really happened to Jesus when he "died," we would have said, "He didn't even die," or "He really didn't die." We would have seen that he simply passed into glory. Without interruption of the continuity of identity, he passed immediately from the vision of faith, to the simultaneous, once-for-all vision and possession of what he had believed. Real death is for unbelievers and for deniers. With no faith or with denial at that inevitable point of final decision there is nothing to choose. There is no place to go. There is nothing because such a person is nobody by his or her own decision, and is nobody to all the other nobodies. Real death is hell and hell is the only real death.

All of this is said here because that is the point and the decision to which our Christian faith brings and keeps us. That is the dimension that Paul speaks of when he says we are "being baptized into his death and resurrection." Death remains not a condition for resurrection, but death is the only point at which resurrection can be entered. In fact, death is the very entrance to resurrection. As it is for Jesus, so it is for us. Death for Jesus is the ultimate achievement of his faith, the ultimate faith decision of self-giving.

Matthew in his account takes Jesus right down to the wire. He comes to the situation of his "death" as an apparent total failure. Everything seems to have gone wrong; even his disciples abandoned him. Matthew doesn't even mention Jesus' Mother and friend John, but says, "Many women were there watching from a distance." (Matthew 27/55.) No wonder he cries, "My God, my God, you too!" "And crying out in a loud voice," not in a whimper, but in a faith mastery of the whole situation, "He *gave up* his spirit." He gave his spirit back to God with the faith certainty "I know you will take me as I am."

This is the decision dimension of what we call death and this decision is faith—a self-movement from the reality of faith to the vision that is glory. In faith, we create our real world. In faith, we make all things and even make God true for us. In death, we come to the vision of God and ourselves and our whole world as it is in the vision of God. As Paul says, "We see as we are seen." We come to God's own vision, and see how good it is to be good enough for God.

In death, Jesus comes immediately to that vision and enters that vision-presence. This is the death-resurrection—the raising-up. The death-resurrection-ascension of Jesus is one entity. We have tried to explain how death is resurrection. Death-resurrection-ascension here, however, is that dimension of the divine initiative by which he is not only received and brought into the presence of God, but the divine initiative by which he is raised-up to the vision of our faith with the promise that this is who we are and who we can become.

The Church is the process of divine initiative and human response. All that the Church is, is what we are in response to God. The Church is the totality of that human response of being raised-up to glory and at the same time raising the Christ up to glory in becoming the people of God that we are called to be. The Church is Jesus in his process of death-resurrection-ascension. The death-resurrection-ascension of Jesus is the present moment of creation. The Church is the present moment of death-resurrection-ascension of Jesus.

At this point, we must return to our premises. The whole universe is brought to the death-resurrection-ascension level of our process, person, presence that is God. Person *presences* self to other, to God. At this point, we must also return to symbol and sacrament. The on-going transcending permanent presence of person to other is symbol and sacrament. In symbol and sacrament, we get in on the experience of other as our own experience. We get in on this experience by faith. We make the experience real by believing.

Jesus, the man, is the sacrament of God. The Church is the sacrament of Jesus, and we are the Church. Faith is the self-movement by which we believe ourselves into and become the real presence that is Jesus. We get in on his faith experience of death-resurrection-ascension as our own real personal experience. The experience is immediate, without medium or instrumental cause, and above all, is not vicarious. The Church is our own immediate personal experience of the death-resurrection-ascension of Jesus.

I have tried many times to teach death-resurrection-ascension of Jesus in the light of new theological insights with the awareness that there is a lot of unlearning to be done. I have not yet decided whether it is easier to do the painful unlearning before or after the affirmation of what the resurrection really is. The following is what the resurrection is not:

1. The resurrection is not the reanimation of the corpse. In the phrase "resurrection of the body" in the creed, "body" does not mean "body" vs "soul" as in the Greek image of person, but "body" means person-present, the body-person of Christ that we are, being raised up in the presence of God.

2. Scripture and the gospel do not speak of resurrection in our Greek cultural image of person. "He is risen" does not say his soul has returned to his body and he is revived, he has gotten his old life back again, or he has come back to life again. It is a proclamation that he lives. He has a new life in a new body. He is raised up to the glory of the Father.

3. All doctrinal affirmation and insistence notwithstanding, the resurrection of Jesus is not "physical." Early doctrinal affirmations say that Jesus rose physically. Insisting that it was "physical" was the only way that it could be made real in the cultural image and in the categories that were the cultural premises in which the early proclamations were made.

4. The "body" of the resurrection is not the "glorified" physical body somehow transcending the trammels of the physical laws of time and space.

5. In short, resurrection does not mean that he got his old life back in a new transfigured, glorified body capable of beatific vision.

6. "On the third day " does not mean primarily on the third calendar day, nor does it mean after some delay. On "the third day" is a cultural reference to the dark of the moon; it is

an affirmation drawn from the certainty that the moon will inevitably return. So with the resurrection, it is sure to happen.

Furthermore, in a culture far less frenetic and impatient than we are, "on the third day" meant right now without delay. After all, the third day is always the day after tomorrow. Then too, as we mentioned earlier, there had to be enough time to establish evidence for historical credibility that he was really dead and buried.

7. The soul of Jesus did not wait in "limbo" until it could be reunited with his body because there was no other place it could go, and because the "gates of heaven" were closed until Jesus died. With these false premises, even he couldn't go to heaven because he had not gotten back his glorified body which he needed for the beatific vision. All of these were theological conclusions drawn from the bad premise. The bad premise was the Greek body-soul image of person and these conclusions are an attempt to accommodate resurrection to the "human nature" of Jesus in that Greek image. God's covenant with his people is real and unconditional. The old covenant does not say "I will be your God, *if* you will be my people." It is the affirmation, "I am your God and you are my people." In Mary's faith and in the life and death of Jesus, the old covenant is a complete success. Finally, in Jesus' total faith we have achieved the birth, the baptism, the generation by which we are really and fully named as sons and daughters of God. The new covenant is simply the old covenant fulfilled. New testament or covenant, the resurrection, is out of the tomb at Calvary, not out of the crib at Bethlehem.

There now follows what the resurrection really is.

1. Most important, the resurrection is mystery in which the whole mystery of God and creation is centered.

2. The reality which counts and matters most about the resurrection is that which is made true by those who believe in the Risen One. The mystery is person-present who must be named not described.

3. "Resurrection" is not a good word for the mystery. The mystery is person-present in an on-going process in which those who believe in him enter the presence and live in the presence of God as most favored sons and daughters, and are the body of his presence to the Father.

4. The Risen One is *cosmic person* of whom Paul speaks as "first born from the dead" in whom all people and the whole world are "*named*," come into their own, come into their inheritance and possession of their God and his universe.

5. The death-resurrection-ascension of Jesus is one entity. His death is his resurrection, is his ascension. For our vision and faith experience there are these three aspects of the one event revealed sequentially to accommodate our faith and to reveal the event in its on-going process in us where the reality of the event is taking place.

6. In his resurrection Jesus is the same but "new" person, with a new life in a new body.

a) "Same but *new* person. In death-resurrection there is a continuity of identity without interruption in which the same person is transformed from person of faith to person of vision of glory.

b) New person with new real presence is not only living, but real person is (be's) life (I am the life.) It is passage from mortal to immortal, passible to impassible with identity possessed and secured.

c) In a new body, new person with new life in a new body are really three aspects of the same mystery. "Body" really means person-present. Body is the identification of person-present and it is the mode or the manner of presence. The body is not the instrument or means by which the person is present. The body is the presence itself. The body aspect of the resurrection is the blind spot in our culture and in our traditional theology because we start with our Greek image of body and soul, and with our Greek categories of matter and spirit. Body and soul is a flawed and inadequate image of person to begin with and is grossly inadequate and even incompatible with and contradictory to the faith vision of the resurrection. It is simply bad language for the proclamation of the mystery and bad language for the theological search into the mystery. We must not think of the resurrection in terms of human spirituality that means, "I have a soul." The soul or spirit is supposed to be the subject doing the being or possessing. If "I have a soul" the "I" is somehow prior to the "having" and to the soul. The soul or spirit is not the subject. We must not say "I have a soul," but rather "I am, I *be* spirit," I am body-person-spirit-presence, I am a spiritual or spirit-body. The body that I am is my presence to God, to all other, to the whole world in this phase of my existence in which, by my on-going faith decision in a process of self-creation and self-determination, I will achieve a permanent transcending identity and presence which is the vision of God. The body that I am makes it right for me to be where I am and who I am. My body is my belonging. My body is the dynamic of my othering spirit presence. My body is the sacrament *of*, the sacrament *that is*, the person-presence that I am.

All of this is said here because all that the resurrection is, is within this person-presence-process. In fact, it is the whole person-presence, the God-to-us and us-to-God creative process, brought to the fullness of its final stage. It is the cosmic return to God. We are there but we are still in process; it has all been done but there is more to do. We have entered the mystery but there is always new entry in the faith process that constantly enters deeper and deeper into the mystery presence that is God.

At this point, it must be emphasized also, that the human person is primarily a corporate process. There has been a tragic loss in our awareness of the glory in our share in the glory of the resurrection because we have measured it within the limits imposed by our Greek cultural image of person. There is an even greater loss that in that same Greek image we have measured it in the Greek primacy of the individual. In that same way, the first truth about being human is that we are a corporate person. The first truth about the body of the resurrection is that it is corporate. Our theology has failed so miserably here that we have made the glorious proclamation of the early creed, "We believe in the resurrection of the body" to mean reconstruction and reanimation on the last day, with the implication that we will have to wait until that last day to get in on the resurrection of Jesus. "We believe in the resurrection of the body" is an affirmation of the present glory, that we are the body of the resurrection, that the resurrection of Jesus is what we are, no more, no less—its total is in us. It is the present happening, the process that is the Church. Our God is *Abba*, father of our Lord Jesus Christ, who is raising him up in glory in us. Given the unfinished dimension of our humanity, he has scarcely begun to see his glory.

We have been so confused about this that we actually have given Jesus Christ three presences and in effect three bodies. In this confusion, the first body is that which was reanimated in a glorified state and with which he emerged from the tomb "physically" and in which he has physically ascended into heaven. The second body is the body by transubstantiation or consubstantiation with which and in which a real presence for us is achieved in the tabernacle under consecrated species. The third, which is really the first and total presence, we have reduced to a figure of speech and have said that one could speak of the Church *as if* it were the body of Christ. In this image or metaphor, we have created two entities: one, Christ the Head; the other, the Church, the Body of which he is the Head. Likewise we have made Christ the Bridegroom, the Spouse of the Church, rather than the Christ, the Church, the Spouse of God. We have made Christ the Risen One, and the Church an effect or product of the resurrection, not the very body of resurrection itself.

In this matter, it is regrettable that in our culture we disdain images as being adequate only to a point and somehow less than the real thing. Images are forbidden in dogmatic pronouncements. If used as "Body of Christ" in dogmatic definitions about the Church, it is with disclaimer and warnings that the word "body" is *only* an image, but acceptable, as far as it goes. Images are beautiful faith words. They evoke experience and imagination. They are open ended, without limit and defy definition. Here again, we have reduced the resurrection by making it a "teaching of the Church," like we have made the "divinity of Christ" a teaching of the Church. We have in effect put the Church before Christ and made the Church a teacher "about" the Christ and God, rather than having the Church be the real Christ presence and sacrament of God teaching his people. The Church is the real presence of the Father raising up his son in glory in us, to us and for us. Anything less than this is not the church and there is nothing more than this. It is the total cosmic reality. For this reason, it takes image to proclaim it, because the mystery defies definition.

Out of the Old Testament into Mary and into Christ, the Church emerges into the image of spouse. This is a most beautiful image out of the most beautiful human experience of believing and being believed in, of loving and being loved. The believers in and lovers of God that write their faith-love experience in the scripture found "spouse" of God to be the best image in which to proclaim their identity and their faith experience of union with God, achieved by resurrection faith, that is, by being the Risen One being glorified for his faith-love of his *Abba*-Father.

When this good news was proclaimed to the Greek culture, the Greek accepted it on their own terms and only to the point that it could be made compatible with their own ideas and contained in their categories. As we have seen they made the resurrection the reanimation of the corpse. Because for the Greek, "idea" and "image" are identical and synonymous, scriptural images are valid only to the point that they can be defined and explained by the systematical rules of rational logic and contained in rational categories. From that point on through the history of the Western Church as now, we have trouble with the image of "spouse," and even have been embarrassed at the reference. As there has been the cultural compulsion to remove anything and everything sexual from the human origin of Christ, there has been the compulsion to make the image of "spouse" asexual or non-sexual. Worst of all, it could never be admitted as image for Jesus himself—which it really is. Our theology out of its gratuitously assumed culture premise has not allowed "appreciation" of the Scripture but only "interpretation," which will not allow the man Jesus to be any kind of "spouse."

Out of this compulsion, we have a whole history of a theology that makes the Church the *Spouse of Christ*, (possessive genitive), speaking of his care and his concern for his Church. We have set this up in a man-woman, male-female relationship, but have cautiously removed even any suggestion of anything sexual in the union, and "defined" the image in such a way as to exclude positively any possibility of such reference. In this process out of the same compulsion, the image "virgin" has become a defined *term* and has been violated by being denied its first real meaning of total fidelity.

The Church is not the spouse of Christ but the spouse of God. Jesus in his resurrection is received by God as spouse. We are his body, the body that is his resurrection. He is us and we are him. We are spouse of God, that is the Church; that is what it means to be Church-Spouse of God.

In our culture, the word "spouse" has a primary but not exclusive reference to the feminine, but in Scripture, both husbands and wives are spoken of as spouse. However, it is in this primary reference to the feminine that we use the image "spouse" in our talk about God and his Church, which reinforces the projection of God in the masculine image. The primary reference of the word "spouse" is not sexual. Its primary reference is promise: promise made, promise kept, and promise being fulfilled. A spouse is a promise maker and a promise keeper, a promisor and promisee, a believer that can be believed in.

As we are created in the image of God, it is in the images of our human experiences and our human awareness that we speak of our relationship with God and with each other. We will speak of our relationship with God out of the experience and in the image of our relationship with each other. If the image of sexual identity is first in our actual individual and corporate self awareness, we will logically think of God primarily as being sexed and having a sexual identity. Sexism in God language is a cultural problem with theological implications. It is not a problem of faith.

Scripture is written out of the culture of the believing people that wrote it, and the *context* of scripture will inescapably reflect cultural limitations and even cultural prejudices. However, faith, the affirmation of the Scripture about us and God and God and us, will never offend God and his image. In the Old Testament the best things that are said about God are in feminine images. The best believers are cast in feminine images in psalm and canticle, in Mother Maccabee and in a woman named Mary.

The first believer in the New Testament is the man Jesus, proclaimed for his fidelity, not for his masculinity, in the glory of his resurrection, in the image of spouse. This title and image is neither sexist or asexual, but includes and transcends the whole sexual dimension of personal identity. Spouse is the name and the image of person of promise for other who is revelation of God who is totally other for us.

The resurrection is where we meet God and where we meet each other. The first thing about us, where we start to be in God in the resurrection, is that we are one body. If in creation itself the first thing about being human is that we are corporate person, then in the resurrection, which is the new creation, there must be the primacy of the corporate. The greatest and deepest dimension of sin has been the loss of the sense of the corporate, the denial of the corporate, and the failure to achieve any real human corporality in human history.

In our traditional theology in making the resurrection the central Christian dogma and a "teaching of the Church," we have somehow made the "dogma" something less than the "Church" that teaches it, as we have made the Church another entity from the Christ who founded it. The Church proclaims "Jesus lives," but this is not believing in the resurrection. "Jesus lives" really answers no questions, makes no promise, proclaims no urgency. It does no more than somehow validate the authority of Jesus to have made a set of rules for his followers to live by. He had not said, "I will show you the way, tell you the truth, and give you life," but rather, "I am the way, the truth and the life." (John 14/6.) "I am the resurrection and the life, and anyone who lives and believes in me, will really never die." (John 5/25.)

In our system, we have made the resurrection primarily a doctrinal revelation with moral implications and providing moral motivation. This doctrinal-moral distinction and separation is devastating to begin with, but if we must speak from the distinction, the resurrection is first and most of all a moral proclamation. It is the good-news moral manifesto. Now there is everything we need to live for and to live by. Notice that the "we need" is still there, but we have it in hand. It is here and it is us; the total reality of the resurrection is present in those who believe in the Risen One. We are good enough for God. To come to believe in the resurrection is a moral experience and a moral achievement, not just a rational conclusion. To come to believe in the resurrection is an experience of moral urgency to proclaim not who Jesus was and what happened to him, but to proclaim who we are and what has happened to us.

The difference between believing in the resurrection and accepting "Jesus is alive again" is shown in Matthew's account, chapter 28, where the chief priests bribed the guard to say that the disciples carried away the body. They accepted the fact, but denied the resurrection. The resurrection is the point of all and ultimate moral decision. Unbelievers who cannot deny it, ignore it and those who cannot ignore it, deny it. They either deny it or ignore it, but neither ignoring or denying it is neutral. Either way it is a moral decision.

Faith in the resurrection is not only the proclamation of the fact that Jesus is alive again, but it is the proclamation and affirmation of identity of the people who believe in the Risen One. Each gospel is its own unique affirmation of identity of resurrection, "People of the Way." The gospel according to John represents a deepening of the faith awareness of the Christian community that goes beyond the more "primitive" awareness of the synoptics.

Traditionally, John's gospel is spoken of as showing the empty tomb as proof, or at least as sign of the resurrection. Really it is neither. John presents two empty tombs, the tomb of Lazarus and the tomb of Jesus. It is noteworthy that a miracle of the magnitude of the raising of Lazarus appears only in the Gospel of John. The story presents and *explains* the empty tomb of Lazarus. It is the occasion for Jesus's own affirmation of resurrection faith, when he proclaims, "I am the resurrection and the life, and anyone who lives and believes in me will really never die." No doubt the raising of Lazarus from the tomb gave some credibility to his affirmation, but this is not the most important part. Certainly, it was a joy for Martha and Mary and for his friends. In fact, the gospel notes that people from Jerusalem came to Bethany to see this curiosity, a man raised from the dead, not to see the man who raised him.

John's point seems to be to draw a contrast between the two empty tombs. In the real human experience, the people involved could explain the empty tomb of Lazarus. They saw Lazarus. They touched him, talked with him, and ate with him. Of course, his tomb is empty. He is right here alive as he was before, doing the same things. He was the same old Lazarus that he always was.

In contrast, we have the empty tomb of Jesus. Tragically in our own past, we have missed the point and made the resurrection of Jesus another Lazarus, where he got his old life back in his old body, but with one exception, that in the case of Jesus, he did it himself. We have claimed that he raised himself from the dead. In the first place, we are not reducing the human achievement of Jesus, but rather, affirming his human achievement in saying the Father raised him up. Everything that the resurrection is, is within the humanity of Jesus, but we are his humanity, the body of his resurrection. Claims about raising himself up as final proof of his divinity miss the point and are totally inane.

However, there remains the empty tomb of Jesus. What about it? How do you explain it? It can't be ignored or denied. John explains the empty tomb of Lazarus and leaves the explanation of the empty tomb of Jesus to the Christian believer. The Christian believer simply proclaims, "Of course his tomb is empty; he is alive in us." The resurrection of Jesus is not a doctrine that the Church teaches. The resurrection of Jesus is the living reality that the Church is, and in this way the Risen One comes alive and the resurrection is made true by those who believe in him. Where there is no faith, there is no resurrection. There is no Church. Historical reality of the resurrection is not the point; the point is its living reality in us.

All of this is clearly brought out in the resurrection "appearances," or apparitions as proclaimed in the gospels and in Paul's experience on the way to Damascus. The situations and experiences differ vastly in time and place and circumstances, but they all have one thing in common. In each instance, they did not know who he was. They did not "recognize" him until they came to faith, until they came to believe in him. In his resurrection, Jesus has a new life in a new body, and the resurrection is his living human experience in the new body that we are. We are him. He is us. We are the living reality, the living presence to God, the on-going vision and interpresence.

The Church is the faith achievement phase of the process of being raised up in the glory of being son-daughter of the Father.

Here we have the who, what, where, how, when, why of the total human situation. In the resurrection, the whole issue and question and promise of what it means to be human and what to do about it, is presented to us with a vibrant urgency. The man-Jesus, the Risen One is ascended to us, raised up to us, with the promise, this is who we can be. Resurrection faith is the response, "Yes, that's us, that's me; that's who we are." However while we are being raised up we are still in the *dying* phase of being human and we are confronted with our death-resurrection decision in our confrontation and interpresence with others, in the real existential human living situation of joy and sorrow, of pain and suffering, of birth and death. All of these are the human experience of need of other. As resurrection people, we respond to all human needs: admit others to our joys and sorrows and enter the joys and sorrows of others, be a gracious receiver from those who need to give and a gracious giver to those who need to receive.

The resurrection is not just a new state of being. It is a new presence, an interpresence of us and God. "He is risen, He is not here," affirms that he is not in the tomb. It is only the beginning of the message. "He is risen, he is not here in the tomb," but where is he? Faith in the resurrection is the answer, and the faith answer is "Here I am." To believe "in his name" is to assume his identity with the confidence that the believer is the living presence of (that is) the Risen One. We are the real body and the only body that is the resurrection presence to the point that the resurrection is what we are no more and no less.

From the beginning, there have been real believers in the resurrection. The spirit has not failed and never will. Faith is always beautiful. Christian faith always achieves resurrection presence with others with God. While the faith has been good, the theology has been poor and this has been compounded in a culture that has insisted that theological conclusions are the object of faith. Our theology of resurrection has been so poor and unsatisfying that we had to look elsewhere for the "real presence." We contrived a "real substantial" presence under "the appearances" of bread and wine in a ritual. But in spite of the poor theology, we have believed well and have found that God's real presence is in those who believe in him. God's presence to us and ours to him is the resurrection. The people who are this living reality are the living-body-presence. They don't need another presence to be present to.

Ours has been an age of prophetic affirmation and prophetic faith in the corporate dimension of our human personhood over against a cultural, political, sociological premise of the primacy of the individual. History will certainly note this deepening awareness as the beginning of a great movement and the dawn of a new age. The new awareness of the primacy of the corporate liberates humanity from cultural imprisonment in abstract categories and fixed and frozen fundamentalist premises about the primacy of the individual. It opens up to new awareness of the meaning of our Covenant with God, in the resurrection of Jesus, which is itself the covenant.

A covenant is the achievement of a mutual interpresence. Questions of initiator or responder, activity or passivity, active or passive, equality or inequality, superiority or inferiority, finity or infinity, greater or lesser, do not even enter and are of absolutely no consideration or question in the covenant process. It is simply us and God and God and us in a total mutual interpresence. The covenant is brought about always by constant divine initiative. Once it is entered, the initiative and response are mutual. The giving and receiving are mutual. If we are covenanted initiators and givers, God is covenant responder and receiver. A one-sided covenant is a contradiction in terms.

The next liberating movement of the spirit will be to liberate God and us from a one-sided covenant imposed on us by a fundamentalist culture and a fundamentalist theology which has not permitted God to be a covenanted responder or receiver, on the premise that to need to receive from us is beneath the dignity of God and beyond the dignity of man. In *God* there is no condescension in a covenant. By covenant, we are as good for God as he is good for us.

The risen Jesus, who is our covenant with God, has been deprived of a dimension of his glory by this same cultural and theological compulsion to make a one-sided covenant. We refuse to honor receiving as much as we honor giving. While we have pious platitudes about gracious receiving of gifts and expectations about gratitude, we really don't give receivers full covenant status. This is particulary true in our image of the Christ. He is always the worker of the miracle, not the beneficiary. He is much more the giver of the gift, than the receiver even though he has said, "When you do it to one of these least, you have done it to me."

The sin of our age is the corporate sin of condescension to the poor by the arrogant patronizing power of office and of wealth. This follows logically from our cultural premise that disdains any need. We even use the word "needy" as a pejorative term as if to have a need means that there is something missing or something wrong. In our culture, we exalt independence as a primary virtue and reinforce it constantly in our cultural practice and institutions and particularly in our educational process. To starve to death because a person is "too proud" to accept charity is honored as ultimate virtue. Our culture certainly will not accept the covenant reality that our deepest and most authentic possession of anything is to have received it in covenant love from another. Our culture holds rather that the only authentic way to come into the possession of anything, is the fundamentalist "old fashioned" way of *"earning"* it.

Our whole traditional theology of "earning" merit and grace is a contradiction of resurrection covenant. We must bring the freedom and dignity of resurrection covenant to our morality, to all our interpersonal relationships. Our first moral awareness must be that to be human is to be good enough for God, and to be good enough for God is certainly to be good enough for each other. The resurrection is the living covenant of interpresence in the one spirit, where spirit is the gift and the giver.

Who receive him, have him to give. Who give him, have him the gift.

10
CHURCH

ALL THAT IS GOING ON WITH GOD

"WHAT DO YOU THINK OF THE CHRIST, WHOSE SON IS HE?" is the key question in the hearing and understanding of the gospel, and the answer to the question will reveal acceptance or rejection of the gospel message. Given the Resurrection-Ascension of the Christ, the question becomes "What do you think of the Church? Just what is it?" The answer will reveal the character and quality of Christian faith in the gospel or the rejection of the real gospel message. The message comes to the contemporary believer out of a cultural and historical experience that is very confusing.

In times past or present, every believer has to have a prophet to speak the message, a prophet to be a speaker for the believer. A Christian believes that Jesus is the Christ proclaimed in the gospels as "Word of God made flesh," the man who by being the total believer himself is the speaking presence of God. The prophets of old did not "foretell" his coming as much as they "built up" to it in an on-going process of Revelation, and in him the word is fully spoken. The speaking and the believing are in the final phase or stage. In the Death-Resurrection-Ascension of the Christ-prophet, the Word is finally returning to God fulfilled. (Is. 55/11)

The present moment of "Word made flesh," or better, "Word being made flesh" is the Church of Christ, the Church that is Christ. It is the present moment of the giving of the Spirit. The receiving of the Spirit by those who believe is the return to

God. This faith is a self-movement. The believer believes himself or herself into Christ and is given and takes on the Spirit—the person identity—and becomes the body-presence of Christ that is the Church. Whoever, whatever, whenever, wherever these believers are, they are the Church.

The Church that these believers are is alive and well in the real world of real people. The body of Christ that is this Church is the real presence of God to people and of people to God—a living encounter, a real full human experience that can be seen, heard, felt and spoken in the fullness of the language of total human communication and exchange. The Church is real people being really human. In fact, the Church is precisely real people achieving full and authentic human personhood. The church is all that is going on between God and his people.

Process, person, presence is a faith search for self and for God. At this point in our search, we have come to faith in the Risen One. He is proclaimed to us in his Resurrection and lives on in us in his Spirit in the on-going Pentecost which is the Church. We accept him as Word made flesh for us. There has to be a way that we can see and hear him alive and real, know who he is and what he has to say, and hear his invitation and promise. This can be done only by faith. His word is spoken to believers. This word is his gospel—the good news that there is everything for us to live for and everything we need to live by.

Presuming then that we are believers, we look for proclamation of the Gospel promise made credible by real believers who live the gospel way of life, who keep the gospel that they believe and who proclaim it by living it. Given the existential situation of real people in a real world, many other things are entailed in the process of being people of God and Church, but that which makes it Church and people of God is living the Gospel way of life.

The Church emerged from the catacombs and became socially and culturally acceptable in the glory days of the Constantinian Roman Empire. The prevailing culture was essentially

Greek with a Greek body-soul image of man, corresponding to a matter-spirit image of the world. While the Constantinian government reigned supreme and benign in the world of matter, a parallel structure government was set up for the Church to reign in the world of the Spirit. The structure of Church government patterned after the Constantinian Roman governent continues to this day in the hierarchical structure of the Church and has come to be accepted as a divine institution and consequently not subject to change.

We are accustomed to identify Church by those elements that are doctrinal, institutional, structural, ritual, disciplinary and customary as being the essential reality that is the Church. In the one spirit of the Christ, the word *Church* should never be used in the plural form any more than God, Spirit or Christ should be used in the plural form. In spite of the appearance and common perception of many churches, there is one Church. It is not any one of the denominational churches to the exclusion of all others, but it is that transcending spiritual body of the faithful who hear the word of God and keep it.

In our culture, we identify Church and churches by how the members "go to church," the doctrine they hold, their customs and practices and their governing structure. Catholics score high in every category: a very visible hierarchical structure with an infallible pope, mandatory Sunday Mass attendance, Holy Days of Obligation and a celibate clergy. That is how Catholics "go to church," and every denomination and religion has its own way of "going to church."

As we identify churches by how their members "go to church," we have likewise in our culture made "going to church" the principal criterion of fidelity to a religious tradition, whether it be Catholic, Protestant or Jewish. Church authorities and sociologists use "going to church" as the criterion for judging the relative health and well-being of any given Church and of course "going to church" determines the health of any and all of them.

In this matter, it seems that a massive cultural change has already taken place or, at least, is inexorably in the process of change. In our Western culture, "going to church" is no longer the principal criterion of fidelity to a religious tradition— Catholic, Protestant, or Jewish. The reason for this change in cultural practice is the same as for any other cultural change or cultural upheaval. It is a change in "attitude" which simply means a change in values, value criteria, and it reaches much farther than simply "going to church." This whole area is the point of confrontation between liberals and conservatives and between liberation and fundamentalist theology. We will develop the point no further here than to note that the culture is the people. The culture is where people are, how they live, what and where their hopes are, and their aspirations and futilities. The culture is the real living existential human context for the Church. Without the culture, the Church is in a vacuum, isolated and insulated from its mission. The culture is the total context for the proclamation of the Gospel mission. As the written gospel itself is proclaimed to us in and out of a cultural context, so the Church that is the gospel proclamation today must speak credibly in the culture, from the culture, and to the culture. The Church must speak prophetically, embrace and accept everything of the culture that is authentically human and speak out against anything and everything of the culture that denies or contradicts human dignity and human freedom, even if the cultural response is repression or persecution. This confrontation in the culture is the leading edge of the mission of the Church and where hard decisions are made. It is the constant crisis point of urgency and responsibility for church leaders to have the faith vision to move the Church to the final vision.

At this point of decision, fundamentalists avoid the hard decisions by simply condemning the whole culture and cultural process as "secular humanism" and move into an innocuous spiritless vacuum. Liberals and conservatives take their positions at the opposite ends of the cultural spectrum. Their confrontation is itself a valid part of the cultural process and cultural decision for change. The Church should feel right at home because the cultural process is corporate. The peril has been and remains that the Church compromises with or somehow tolerates and accepts premises or values that contradict the Gospel image or the Gospel way of life. This happened tragically when the early Church confronted the Greek culture and accepted the Greek cultural image of person, Greek rationalism and individualism as the criteria for human values. Many of the missionary efforts of the Church have been to be more a culture merchant than gospel messenger. The hierarchical structure of the Church is more a cultural accretion than a divine institution. Canon law that establishes and governs Church structures and processes is written on cultural premises of adversary law.

By divine institution, the Church is human. The Church is sacrament of creative presence—sacrament in which those who believe get in on the real human experience of the Death-Resurrection-Ascension of Jesus in the on-going process of the giving of the Spirit—the becoming of the Body of Christ. Everything the Church is, is the total corporate human response to the creative Fathering-Mothering initiative in which we are being born as the Son-Daughter of God. As the human person is primarily corporate, the Church is primarily corporate. As corporate and individual human person is organic process, the Church is organic process of person-present to-other-to-God. The Church is the mystery of presence and the presence of mystery —the sacrament of the presence that is God. In order to develop and further a theology of Church, we must recall our chapters on faith and on symbol and sacrament and restate our premises. We make symbol-sacrament true by believing it. Symbol-sacrament is the creative achievement of faith in which we achieve transcending permanent presence of person to-other-to-God. Symbol-sacrament is the creative corporate person process.

The scriptural language for institutional creation or founding of the Church is really very good but it has suffered in translation and in theological interpretation. "Thou art Peter" is a creative affirmation of permanent identity of presence. It is not a metaphor or a figure of speech. "You are" is the same creative transitive verb that is in Genesis which means "You be," a creative imperative wording establishing permanent transcending presence, in which the believing Simon-Peter is sacrament of all believers. It is not the establishment of juridical authority but of creative source for the on-going building process.

"I will build my church," not "God will build his church" is an affirmation of the human faith of Jesus. It does not exclude faith in God from the process, but affirms and identifies Jesus' faith in Peter in God, and his faith in God in Peter. It is not an authorization or a delegation but a sacramental establishment. "I will" is not just a future tense, but an affirmation of on-going process of action and works to be done with the assurance that it will be done. It might be rendered "I will be building" or "I will keep on building" or "I will build." "Build" remains a good creative process word in our culture. The word can denote the creative process but without specification of the product. We build a house, a road, a reputation or a friendship and on and on.

In Christ's word in Matthew, "will build" in the Aramaic in which it is first spoken, uses the word "house" as a verb in much the same way that we use the word as a verb meaning to provide a dwelling place. However, in the Aramaic and Hebrew, the word "house" even as a noun is an action word and means a "being lived in" or a presence.

Not too much is lost in the rendering into Greek and Latin because the root of the word used in each instance is the word *oikos* in Greek or *aedes* in Latin, both meaning dwelling place, but in the original Hebrew and Aramaic, it is not a house until it is a "being lived in." In English, the word "build" is so unspecified that it can be a house for the living or a monument for the dead and, regretfully, much of our theology has literally made it a monument for the dead.

"My church," however, remains the main point of trouble and confusion in interpretation. Here we have the classic example of proof-texting. We gratuitously assume that by the word "church," Jesus means the meaning that we have come to give it out of our cultural and theological conclusions and what we would like to have it mean in our theological controversies so we can use it as "proof" for our theological conclusions. It is a way of saying "We are right. The Scripture agrees with us."

The word rendered as "church" in English is *qahal* in Hebrew and Aramaic. *Qahal* is a process word meaning a coming together, an "assembling" more than an "assembly." It includes, also, the dimension of being called to assemble with a purpose and with an urgency to respond. By comparison, our word "church" is dull, flat and colorless.

In Latin, the word is transliterated from the Greek with the same letters and almost the same pronunciation. The word is *ecclesia* and is adopted in the English language in its root form for more formal and theological "church talk." In Greek and Latin, it means an assembly of citizens summoned by a crier—an assembly called for some common civic or political purpose. The early Christians adopted the word for the assembling and assembly of the people of God. The word has the elements of the movement of call and response and purpose.

It is commonly thought and taught that Greek and Latin words ending in *ia, io, ian and ion* are abstract words. This is mostly true as these words are brought into English usage, but it is not true for the original Greek and Latin where such words are process words. This adds beautiful meaning to many such words as *ecclesIA, koinonIA, EucharistIA, revelatIO, and PraesentIA*. There is no compulsion to explain the words in order to have an official interpretation or definition of meaning. On the contrary, they are open and left open to take on their own meaning, open to the faith experience of the people, and open to the mystery that is the kingdom of God.

The gospel remains the most authentic affirmation of the mystery of the Church in which Jesus does not attempt to define or even explain, but says "the kingdom of heaven is like" and proceeds with parables to draw people into the experience of the kingdom of heaven. In the end, Jesus simply says that the community of believers in him, the people of the Gospel way of life, who are willing to risk taking him who is the Word at his word are his Church.

In the earlier days of the Church, there was no compulsion to define what the Church was or to prove its claims. Certainly, there was no proof-texting from Scripture to prove any doctrine, in the sense that we have done it, since the thirteenth century through the Council of Trent and Vatican I. In the early days, the presence of The People of the Way was their affirmation of identity, which simply said "Here we are." The gospel message we have written is the affirmation of our identity and an invitation to all people to join with us to enter the mystery of the kingdom of God. They spoke from a sense of presence because of their awareness that they, the community of believers, were the living presence of the Risen One. The same promise of presence is the final words of the Gospel. "Behold I-with-you-am all the days of your life." (Matthew 28:18)

We have considered the so-called Petrine text from Matthew 16 not to explain or to define its meaning, but to open it to the mystery of presence that it affirms. The gospel closes on the same theme but with different words. The text is Matthew 28/18-20 and opens with declaration of identity. After the Resurrection, having met his disciples on the mountain in Galilee, he declares "All authority (power) is given to me, in heaven and on earth. Go therefore, make disciples of all the nations; baptize them in the name of the Father, and of the Son, and of the Holy Spirit, and teach them to observe all the commands I gave you. And look, I am with you always, yes to the end of time." This text has suffered much of the same fate as the Petrine text. It has been proof-texted, literally, to death to prove the authority and power of the Church in the image of the Council of Trent and Vatican I. It has been used to prove a special providence that makes the Church infallible, all of which is completely foreign and even contradictory to the image of Church out of which the Church wrote the gospel in the first place.

The Church writes the gospel and the gospel which the Church has written can hardly be adduced as any kind of *proof* for the Church that has written it. The gospel is in the true sense the "teaching" of the Church. It is the message, the good news, the promise of a way of life that brings joy and happiness and fulfillment of human purpose. It is an invitation to a way of life with "us." "Try it, you'll like it." It is a promise of "salvation," but salvation here and now, not only hereafter. "Salvation" is "well-being," from the Latin "*salve*" which is the word used for friendly greeting and for "salutation" in a letter to a friend. The Church did not write the gospel on the premise that "this world and this life is only a vale of tears" and "trial and tribulation." This is where the Resurrection takes place, where we enter the tomb to enter the Resurrection. The tomb is here. Entering the tomb is baptismal entering into the Resurrection process and grief, sorrow and what seems to be death is the human faith experience of entering the joy and the vision of the glory of the sons and daughters of God. All that the Church is, it is as the human faith response to the word and promise of God.

The Petrine text must be "appreciated" and "interpreted." We have tended to only interpret it to prove our counter reformation theological conclusion. The text opens with the faith affirmation, "All authority (power) in heaven and on earth is given to me." This is the affirmation of the human achievement of the total creative dominion promised us in Genesis "Take it and keep it." Jesus affirms that he has achieved the vision of Genesis, that he has taken possession of creation and tells his disciples to take it from there. "All *exousia* has been given to me." In the text, the key word is "authority" or "power." The key to the appreciation or interpretation of the text is in the "original" Genesis, "Take it and *keep* it." "Keep" does not mean simply to take possession of and to secure and maintain ownership. It means to accept it and to assume responsibility for its well-being (salvation), to bring about its God-given purpose. It speaks of the establishment of authority and power at its creative source by covenant, not authority and power "over" as interpreted by our cultural adversary law in which image we have cast the "authority of the Church."

The Greek word used in the text for "authority" and power is *exousia. Exousia* does not mean power and authority, but in the Greek and in the Latin equivalents, it is inescapably "official." This is borne out and reinforced by the language of our theology and canon law. We speak of the "official" teaching of the Church as the ultimate statement of faith. We speak of *clerical and hierarchical "office" and especially of the "office" of the papacy.*

This is further reinforced by our traditional cultural theological premise that the primary teaching function of the Church is to make doctrine and dogma and that faith is "submission" to the teaching "office" of the Church. We have a painful memory of four hundred years of so-called reformation controversy about who has the real teaching office in the Church. It is the wrong question. We must all begin to ask "Just what is a *teaching of the Church?*"

The words of the Petrine text are a good place to start to look for the answer because the gospel text is the statement of the self-awareness of the early Church, the primordial awareness of mission and sense of urgency to proclaim the good news and promise to all people of all time, in every place and in every culture. The proclamation must always be a credible promise for those who are willing to believe. Whatever that is and however that is done is the teaching and the teaching "authority" of the Church.

"In heaven and on earth" is an affirmation of the totality and adequacy of the power given. It is not the affirmation of a bi-level, two-tiered structure of "up there" and "down here" out of our culture, as if the Church were acting as "official" agent of God "up there." "In heaven and on earth" is an image out of the Aramaic Hebrew culture in which it was spoken, and it is an affirmation of the total cosmic dimension of power and authenticity at the creative source.

"Is *given* to me" means he has achieved it, but it is given. He has come into the possession of the power, which is Spirit, and now it is his to give. This is an affirmation of the humanness of Christ and his Church, that it is an unending process of giving and receiving and giving the Spirit.

"Going therefore" says many things. In the giving of his Spirit, it says first and most of all, "You go and be me." This is the mission that the Church is, the sacrament of Christ who is sacrament of God.

"Make disciples of all nations." "Make disciples" is a much better rendering than "teach" because it is much more specific and implies an interpersonal relationship and process and a faith commitment. In this process, a disciple is not just a student learning content from a teacher. A disciple is a person committed to follow a master, to learn by doing, to learn a way of life by living it. We are well aware of the validity of the method which we call experiential learning. The Gospel invitation to discipleship is "Come, follow me." "I am the way, learn of me." It is an invitation to covenant, in which the disciple is first chosen by the master and the disciple freely chooses to follow and go all the way, even unto death. To "make disciples" means to invite and to lead to faith in Jesus Christ. To believe in "his name" is truly to assume his identity by receiving his Spirit, and in him to enter covenant with his Father. God offers no covenant to any one person or nation or people to the exclusion of any other. Hence, "make disciples of all nations" means make covenant, but it is one and the same covenant for each and for all. There can be no privilege or immunity for any one, superior or inferior. Covenant does not demand submission. Covenant transcends equality because equality measures and all who are equal are reduced to the least common denominator. Adversary law lauds equality as supreme and makes equality the measure of justice. A disciple "hungers and thirsts" after covenant *justice* in which every believer has his or her own total possession of the Spirit. It is a possession shared, not by division, but because each believer's own possession is total and the Spirit gives himself to each precisely by giving himself to all.

It is at this point, that there is injustice and sin against the Spirit. A believer is always a totally dependent receiver who by covenant is expected to be a total giver. The first injustice and sin against the Spirit is the common presumption that there are those in the Church that are no longer disciples—that they somehow have graduated. While many of these may think they know it all or have no need to know any more, this is not their greatest sin. Their greatest sin is to think they have outgrown discipleship by being invested with "teaching authority" and that now they are givers in their own right without any need to receive. To rise above discipleship would be the contradiction of rising above covenant. Discipleship with Jesus is simply our side of covenant with God.

While the Church is and will always be a community of disciples, the mission imperative remains "Make disciples of all nations." It must be a process both of becoming disciples and making disciples. Becoming disciples and making disciples are the same work of the same Spirit. How this can be and how it can be achieved is probably the most urgent question, issue or problem confronting the Church today. It is the problem of ministry, which is the problem of how does the Church make disciples. Making disciples means much more than teaching doctrine or Christian education.

Discipleship is ministry and ministry is discipleship. Making disciples and becoming disciples is the same process. The Gospel states that Jesus told his disciples to "make disciples." In this mission statement, the "eleven" are called "disciples" with no reference to any special or exclusive power or privilege. Those eleven happen to be the eyewitnesses to the Death-Resurrection event and will credibly establish the event in human history, and it is by this discipleship that they will give the Spirit. These eyewitness disciples have grounded and founded the on-going Death-Resurrection event which is the Church, in which it remains true that no disciple is greater than any other disciple except by being the least.

In our history, there has been so much emphasis on discipleship as learning the doctrine and on doctrine and dogma as the object of faith, that we have made ministry a kind of social service in the Church or the specific function of "preaching." We use the words *preacher, minister, priest, clergyman* as title, generally implying special class or privilege meriting the additional title, "Reverend," which in Latin means "one to be revered or feared." All of this is reinforced in Church structures and practice that have clerics or clergymen and lay people. The Presbyterians certainly had the right idea, but made the mistake of trying to give everybody the title of "presbyter" or priest and have discovered that, when equality is the issue, there is always going to be somebody more equal.

It is regrettable that the word "lay" has come to be used to designate the non-cleric or the non-professional, which is not only a pejorative classification but a declassification to the lowest rank, when there should be no rank to begin with. In the early Christian community whose language was Greek, they used the word "*laos*," which means "the people," as the word to speak of themselves as the People of God, the People of the Way. They simply thought of themselves as the people who believed, who got their identity and their dignity by faith in the gospel which committed them to minister to each other's needs. In recent years in all the churches, there has been a serious attempt to "involve the lay people" in ministry and administrative decisions. Since the Second Vatican Council, this has been called *"collegiality"* in the Catholic Church and the word has taken on some interesting meanings. In the early post-conciliar days, it was called collegiality when the bishops began to talk to each other and the Pope began to listen to the bishops even though they were "only advisory" in final decisions. Gradually, the real competence of the laity began to be recognized and lay people were admitted to parish councils, to liturgical functions and to minister to the needs of the people of God. Progress has been slow and acceptance has been grudging and reluctant on the part of both clerics and laity. Diocesan and parish councils remain "only advisory," "Lay ministers" are regarded as surrogate or substitute priests by both clergy and laity; women are regarded as surrogate or substitute men. With all of this, the greatest impediment is the cultural malaise which keeps people comfortable and uninvolved in the fundamentalist acceptance of the ultimate validity of the institutional status quo and the fundamentalist acceptance of "absolute authority" and "blind obedience," in which people and clerics enjoy the comfort and the security of no risk in having someone else make all the decisions for them. "All authority is given to me" easily becomes "Absolute authority is given to me."

The authority problem compounds the ministry problem mostly because those in authority do not recognize authority as a ministry or government as a service, because if authority is power, it is impossible to make a work of power a real ministry. The problem is generally seen as a problem of concession, compromise, permission, and authorization. We must solve the problem by removing it and answer the question by invalidating it. We remove the problem by faith, by being willing to be and to remain disciples, and by removing and rejecting all elements of structure and procedure that give titles and privilege that somehow graduate the chosen ones from "discipleship" to "authority." We remove the problem by *keeping* the faith, by living and keeping the covenant that the faith is and not denying the covenant by reducing it to the categories of adversary law. "The truth will set you free" is a covenant promise. If a minister needs permission for ministry, he or she is really not free. If a minister needs official authorization through "proper channels," he or she is not really free. Adversary laws give permission. Covenant sets people free; a person does not need permission to be a disciple.

Discipleship is a covenant that sets the disciple free to live and to act "in the name" of Jesus Christ. We come again to the creative dynamic of symbol and sacrament. "In the name of" means in the person of, with the identity of. When we receive his Spirit, we are "in his name," we are him. It comes very clear in Luke, chapter nine, that those who were called to discipleship showed how much they had yet "to learn of him" when they had an argument about which of them was the greatest. Jesus took a little child, who is the image of a true believer in being comfortable in being dependent, and said, "Anyone who welcomes this child in my name, welcomes me, and anyone who welcomes me, welcomes the One who sent me. The least among you all is the one who is greatest." At this point, John, who was in the argument about who was the greatest, tried to justify himself and to protest his loyalty by saying that they had encountered an unauthorized minister and said, "We saw someone driving out devils in your name and because he is not with us we tried to stop him." But Jesus said to him, "You must not stop him. Anyone who is not against you is for you."

The unauthorized exorcist was obviously quite effective; he was really healing hurting people. "By their fruits you shall know them" is the Gospel criterion for authenticity, not a certificate issued by a proper authority. The Spirit does not establish a structure of levels of authority, but the Spirit is a given and giving presence that brings everyone who receives and gives the Spirit into the presence that is God for whom there is no level or measure except that the measure of giving is the measure of receiving. Ministry is sacrament, immediate interpresence. Ministry is not by delegation, authorization or by third party instrumental causality.

All of this is said with an acute awareness of the problems confronting Church ministry in the real existential situation of ministering to real people in the living human condition. We are aware that credibility demands competence, that effectiveness demands order and efficiency. We are aware that effectiveness in ministering to contemporary human needs requires professional skills and competence and organization, but the best professional skill is not a ministry of healing unless it is a work of compassion, and the most skillful teaching and preaching is not a ministry of the Word unless the teacher or preacher is Word made flesh by being a true believer.

Ordination is not authorization or empowerment. (See chapter on sacrament.) Ordination is the sacramental process in which the ministers or preachers present themselves to the community with a sense of urgency and mission and are received and accepted by the community for the gift and word that they bear. In the true Church of Christ, there can be no rule, regulation or law that prevents or excludes any believers from ministering or proclaiming and preaching the word he or she believes, or that prevents any persons of compassion from doing any of the work of healing in the name of Jesus. "You must not stop them" (Luke 9:50) for any reason, not because they haven't gone to the right schools, not because they haven't paid their dues, not because they don't belong to the right club, and most of all, not because they are "only women."

It is true that there must be a valid function and role of authority in the Church. The primary function of authority is to minister; the primary quality of authority is credibility. Authority is obeyed by being believed in. Those in charge of the community must minister by providing credible ministers to serve the needs of the faithful. In the contemporary socio-cultural situation in which the human needs are identified and served by trained professionals, Church ministry is likewise a profession with established standards of competence and excellence. However, while these generally accepted professional standards are part of the criteria of credibility for the priest or minister of the Church, the primary criterion is personal faith in the word of God and a love commitment to serve the "poor in spirit." While it is the responsibility of Church authority to provide credible ministry for the Church, that authority itself has a larger responsibility for its own credibility, and must not lose its credibility by making incredible exclusions from ministry of competent credible believers because of their sex.

The Church must be credible where it is believed in and where it is belonged to. In our theological tradition, we have made the Church credible on paper and in theory, which was easy to do because we made the Church a divine institution that people belonged to. The Church was something of another world that was somehow better than the people that belonged to it. We are starting to say that the Church is the people, but we remain a long way from really knowing its meaning and implications. The Church as the people of God is still very much on paper and in theory. "Joining the Church" is still somehow joining a third entity institution that other people belong to. It is still not joining the human community that the other people are. "Belonging to the Church" still has much of the connotation of being possessed by the Church, of "submission" to teaching and governing authority—something like paying the price for the privilege of belonging.

We have worked on the fallacy that the Church is perfect and without sin, but people fail to measure up to the requirements of membership. The Church is not a static, fixed institution. The Church is the process of people being people, the process of people being human, and the process of people being people to each other to God. The Church is no more and no better than the people who are the Church. The people who are the Church have a vision of what they can be and believe that they are a people of promise. The Church is the achievement phase of the process. If we were already perfect, there would be nothing to promise. If we were without limit, we could not love or be loved. If we were without sin, we could not be given the holiness of being forgiven; we can "belong" only where we have needs and where we are needed.

People can't really "belong" in or to an authoritarian structure, because an authoritarian structure not only denies real needs of people, but imposes false needs. There is a long history of authoritarianism in the Church structure itself and also in institutional structures and practices within the Church. Liberation theology is in itself a movement away from authoritarianism in theology itself and is also an affirmation of the true freedom of the Spirit in Church structure and practice. The reactionary fundamentalist law and order backlash in Church, society and politics of the 1980's is already beginning to wane and lose credibility. Liberation theology is here to stay and will be heard as the prophetic voice of our cultural age. We hope that, in its turn, it will remain liberating and give way to the new prophet when the next new age appears.

The most common offense of authoritarianism is self-righteousness. Authoritarians arrogate power and privilege to themselves and consider themselves to be the source of the gift and well being that the law of God gives to those who receive it. Self-righteousness is the ultimate lie, the ultimate sin, the unforgivable sin—the sin against the Spirit. Self-righteousness is the contradiction of faith, the contradiction of the word, the self-affirmation of no need of any other or of God. Such a person cannot serve or be served and such authority excludes any belonging. Self-righteous Church authority is patronizing, prevents and actually forbids real belonging to the Church.

The Church is simply the final phase of the creative people process. It is the present moment of the Resurrection.

To become fully aware of the mystery that is the Church, we need a deep conversion. We must overcome the limitations of many of our cultural premises. The first step in the conversion is to establish the primacy of the corporate, what it really means to be the Body that is Christ. We are the Word made Flesh and the more we realize and believe it, the more true it becomes. The most devastating of our past errors has been and remains our emphasis on individual salvation in which we consider that the ultimate purpose of Church membership is to save our individual souls for a next life—to "go to heaven." "I must save my soul even if everybody else goes to hell." This is rife with fallacy and error. The urgency is always for the authenticity of the present moment; there is no future without it. There are no solos in salvation. If everybody else goes to hell, I will inevitably go with them. We must not look to the Church to do it for us. This is why Church authority becomes arrogant and self-righteous. This is the appeal of fundamentalist evangelism—a false promise of easy religion and instant salvation, that it will be done for you if you join up and pay your dues.

The Church is people involved in the mystery of the saving presence of God in Jesus Christ. This is the mystery of the resurrection. The resurrection is not something that happened to Jesus two thousand years ago from which we derive benefit. The resurrection is happening in us who enter the process by believing ourselves into it. It is a cosmic process, the present moment of creation. It is the Church. It is happening right here where we live and breathe, where we believe and love. It happens and exists in our interpersonal relationships, in our sacramental interpresence. The Spirit we give up, to and for each other, is the present moment of the death of Jesus. The faith that we have in each other in God is the creation of the body of the resurrection of Jesus that we are as his Church, and the faith-love life of the Christian community is the ongoing giving of the Spirit that is holy, which is the Church.

11
SPIRIT

GOD ALIVE AND WELL IN US

THE DEATH, RESURRECTION, ASCENSION OF JESUS are really one entity, but by necessity are revealed to us sequentially and appear to be a series of events culminating in the final event of Pentecost, the giving of the Spirit. What seems to be a series is really one ongoing event in which his death is his resurrection, is his ascension, is the giving of the Spirit. The "giving up" His Spirit which is his death is the same giving as the giving of the Spirit which is Pentecost. It is the giving of the Spirit to God to us, to us to God, by which and in which we are the body of his resurrection.

It is the present moment of the ongoing creation event spoken of in a variety of terms—"the sending of the Spirit," "the coming of the Spirit," and "the descending of the Spirit"—each and all of which somehow describe the "to other" movement and abiding presence of God. It starts in creation. It is the same Spirit that "hovers" over the waters in the creation account and which gives identity to all that is called from the unpresence that is chaos by being called and named into the presence that is God. It is the Spirit, the Ruah, the breath, with which God "breathes" Adam, "shaping him from the soil of the ground, breathing the breath of life into his nostrils and man becomes a living being..." (Genesis 2/7) Adam comes alive with the life of God. God has given Adam the Spirit and Life that is God. He is created in the image of God.

It is at this point that we begin the devastating process of denying God into our image rather than believing ourselves into the image of God. We do this by establishing our cultural image of matter-spirit, body-soul composite as the premise of our faith and of our theology. Thus the Spirit given is "only created" and "only human" and "only analogous" to the Spirit that is God. It becomes Spirit in the category of "Spirit" versus matter and is further denied by being defined by what it is not. It is not matter and cannot be perceived by the senses. The most devastating of all the attempts at definition by category is reduction to the category of analogy which makes the human spirit or soul "something like" but "vastly different" from the Spirit that is God. "Image" of God has been made synonymous with "analogy" and has been made to mean "something like, but vastly different" from God of whom we are image. Our cultural and theological premises prevent and forbid that image means identity, with the insistence that we can be no more than "only human," and "image of God" can be no more than analogous and that any more than analogy with God would be an arrogant blasphemous presumption.

Creation is covenant. Covenant is total giving with the expectation that the giving itself is the "measure" of the return. No less is to be given back than is first given. In the language of Genesis, "*ruah*" or "spirit" or "breath" are not just a sign or a proof of life as we would say, "He is breathing; he is alive." In this language "spirit-breath" is life itself. The language says that God breathed Adam and Adam comes alive with the *Ruah-Breath-Spirit* that is the Life that is God.

The covenanting, fathering, creating God would not and could not have breathed a life that was less or only analogous to the Life that he is. To do such would not have been covenant and would not have been God.

The Spirit God gives Adam in creation covenant is the total Spirit that God is. In the covenant, Adam has the Spirit by receiving it. To be Adam is to be receiving the Spirit and to be God is to be giving the Spirit and the Spirit given is not less than the God who gives it. Covenant is achieved when Adam comes into the possession of the Spirit that He/She is by giving the Spirit back to God in giving It to others. This is the failure and sin of Old Adam. He rejected covenant by refusing to give his spirit back to God. Adam and his world became a spiritless, desolate, nameless wasteland at the bottom of the pit longing for the return of the Spirit.

When all seems lost, there is hope against hope. When all have failed, there finally comes a true believer, a true covenantor and the return of the Spirit. "You have found favor with God and the Holy Spirit will come upon you, and the power of the Most High will overshadow you, and your child will be holy and called the son of God." This announcement is in no way a description of the physiological manner of conception and birth, but is is an affirmation of the return of the Spirit to the true believer. The Holy Spirit is the Spirit that is God received and possessed by New Adam. The New Adam, the Christ, comes into the possession of the given Spirit by giving His Spirit back to God by giving it to others and for others, by being totally the man for others.

In no instance does the gospel say "He died" or that "He was killed." The gospels do not deny or preclude this element in the account but they affirm much more. Matthew says, "But Jesus, again crying out in a loud voice, *yielded up* His Spirit." (Matthew 27/50.) Mark says, "But Jesus gave a loud cry, and breathed (spirited) His last." (Mark 15/36.) Luke says, "Jesus cried out in a loud voice saying, 'Father into your hands I commend my Spirit.' With these words He breathed (spirited) His last." (Luke 23/46.) John says, "Jesus said, 'It is fulfilled' and bowing His head He gave up his Spirit." (John 19/30.) Each affirmation in its own way says He freely, on His own, gave his Spirit back to God. That he gave his Spirit back to God is important and significant in understanding what is meant by Holy Spirit in the gospel proclamation of a new covenant. Holiness is what we have in common with God. We are holy with the same holiness by which God is holy. Holy Spirit is God

Spirit, holiness as given to us and possessed by us. It is the Spirit of God, that is Jesus, the Man for others.

Jesus' death is the Man Jesus' return to the Father. Old Adam refused to take possession of the Spirit with which and in which he was breathed and spirited. New Adam has come into the possession of his Spirit by giving it to others to God and now it is his to give.

His death—return to his Father—is creation covenant achieved and fulfilled in resurrection, ascension and given Spirit. His return to the Father is not the end but new beginning at origin. God has to be God. Covenant has to be fulfilled and the best that God can be and can do for his son will be done. Words fail, but this returned son must be duly rewarded. Whatever this is, is his resurrection.

Jesus' return to his Father is his total love for us, and he will be properly rewarded for giving up his Spirit for us. In this resurrection, he is the same but new person, given a new life in a new body, and how better can he be rewarded than by being given those whom he has so loved as the new body of his new life. In giving of his Spirit, he is being given identity of presence with those whom "He has loved to the end." Love to the end 'eis telos' does not mean only that he persevered and did not quit, it means he took human love all the way, as far as it could go. "Greater love than this no one has, that a person lay down his life for his friends." (John 15/13.) He gives his Spirit for us and we are given to him by the Father as the body-person worthy and good enough for him to give his Spirit. This is the Church, the ongoing loving giving process of person inter-presence that is holiness.

In our traditional theology, the doctrinal conclusions about the Holy Trinity have become the premises for all discussion about Church, sacrament and holiness. In these premises, the role and function of the Spirit is set up as the sanctifier and the giver of the gifts of God. The Holy Spirit is likewise set up as the protector and guide for the Church with an abiding "over"-presence, keeping the Church from harm, and leading the Church on its way. Theology has cast the Holy Spirit in a trinitarian role which has made the Spirit not only third person but third party, a kind of an agent for the godhead. All the doctrinal affirmations and assurances about person, notwithstanding, it has been difficult to bring believers to a level of familiarity and easy comfort with the Spirit as real person-present. All the theology about gifts and fruits of the Holy Spirit has made the Spirit the giver more than the gift.

God is the giver and the gift. The Holy Spirit is God given and received. The Holy Spirit is the human spirit which is God received and is not less God or less than God being received. To be human is to be Spirit given and Spirit received to become Spirit possessed by being Spirit given. At this point, our traditional body-soul image presents a great obstacle and limitation and that is, that in our image, being Spirit or spiritual is only part of being human. To be human is to be totally Spirit and spiritual. To refuse to be Spirit is to refuse to receive the gift that God is and gives; it is to refuse to be human and that is sin. To be human is to be holy. Holiness is not just a human quality or a kind of option. Holiness is God being received, and that is holy human spirit.

Here, we meet the deepest human reality and encounter the deepest human mystery. We meet that about ourselves which is bigger than we are, and we can enter the presence and the mystery only by faith. Our traditional theology of Spirit has not really been faith. We have measured the mystery by our reason and called it mystery because we couldn't explain it. We have tried to dissect the mystery and force it into our ontological categories which we have considered adequate to explain and to account for all of reality. The result has been a long list of inanities about consubstantial, coequal, same nature, procession from, etc. In fact the body-person, that is the Church, was itself a contradiction of the Spirit in a bitter fight between the East and the West about the procession of the third person from the first and the second, or only from the second. The *"filioque"* infighting about the theology of the procession of the Holy Spirit was itself a contradiction and a denial of the unifying presence of the Spirit that is God given and received, which presence is the Church.

We must not get lost about being lost or inane about being inane and simply affirm that the coming or presence of the Spirit in the Risen One, is what we are to God and God to us. We must not let our contrived categories set limits to the mystery, or let the limits of our categories be the criteria for judgment and decision. We must then boldly affirm first of all that our own experience of being human is the revelation of the Spirit that is God. Our experience of being holy is the revelation of the Holiness of God , and our experience of being holy human spirit is the revelation and the real coming of the Holy Spirit. It is the ongoing Resurrection-Pentecost; it is the Church. The Church is human. It is the glory of the Church to be human, and the Church is Church to the point that it has achieved authentic humanity in the Spirit image of God.

12
SACRAMENT

THE CHURCH AT WORK

FOR FOUR CENTURIES SINCE THE REFORMATION, the different faith traditions in the broad Christian community have compounded the sin of the original division by emphasizing their differences in church teachings and defending the integrity of their own doctrines and practices. The hope of our time is to transcend all differences and to find that we really have a common faith in the word of God. By this transcending harmony, we can achieve a unity in faith and spirit in which no believer needs to compromise the integrity of his or her own faith, but all believers can bring to the common table the integrity of their own faith tradition without compromise or betrayal.

Every Christian body has, by living it, developed a beautiful faith tradition with a unique emphasis and character in the living word of God in their own faith community. The time has come for sharing, for discovering the validity of a faith tradition other than our own and for learning that all believers are inspired by one and the same Spirit. The time has come to learn that a faith tradition is not only a gift received but a gift to be given and that all believers have the privilege and responsibility to proclaim to the world who they are by their own unique traditional possession of one and the same Spirit.

The most significant contribution of the Roman Catholic Church to the current ecumenical blending of the various Christian traditions is the Roman Catholic tradition of faith in sacrament. However, it is another instance of a beautiful faith and a poor theology. The beautiful faith is a *sacramental sense*, a sense of urgency and immediacy of the presence and working of the Holy Spirit in ordinary everyday human activities. It is a sense that the Church is the Spirit in action in which people are bonded in the Spirit to God and to each other.

The poor theology is the result of making the ritual the sacrament, all denials notwithstanding. To defend our undeclared premise that the ritual is the sacrament, we have looked to the gospels for evidence of the institution of the ritual as proof of the institution of the sacrament. We have "defined" sacrament in terms of ritual on all levels of our teaching—from the catechism to dogmatic theology.

For example, we have spoken of baptism as the sacrament in which the pouring of the water and pronouncing the words cause the baptismal effects. We have reduced our sacramental theology to the categories of causality and in effect have said the ritual properly performed causes grace in every category. We have made the ritual the sacrament in applying the hylomorphic theory (all being is comprised of prime matter and substantial form) to the ritual and conclude the integrity and validity of the sacrament by establishing the integrity of the ritual. As in baptism, for instance, the pouring of the water is the prime matter and the simultaneous pronouncing of the words is the substantial form. If the ritual fails by lack of quantity of water, proper pouring, or by failure to say enough of the right words at the right time, the ritual fails by lack of matter or absence of form. Thus, there is no sacrament. The same criteria have been applied to all sacraments. We have made the ritual the sacrament.

If the ritual is the sacrament it is inevitably magic—all disclaimers about "*ex opere operato*" and "*ex opere operantis*" notwithstanding. "*Ex opere operato*" itself becomes the magic formula; "*ex opere operantis*" is the magician. In this whole matter, we have been trapped again in our categories on the premise that our universal metaphysical categories are adequate to explain and to account for all reality, even including the mysteries of faith. The hylomorphic theory is credited as the explanation of the constitution of all being including the Spirit and the works of the Spirit. It becomes a case of completely denying the mystery by attempting to explain it and of contradicting the mystery by attempting to prove it.

It is a theological error to put the word sacrament in the plural form in the first place. Sacrament is the mystery of our interpresence with God in Jesus, a unique living reality. The man Jesus is the sacrament of God; the Church is the sacrament of Jesus. What we are pleased to call "sacraments" are simply the Church at work.

Let us recall here our chapter on symbol. The words *sacrament* and *symbol* are synonymous. We must also recall the language of symbol: the epexegetical genitive in which the word "of" is an affirmation of identity—not of possession—and that all the forms of the word "to be" are transitive verbs. Symbol is not a substitute for reality but symbol is real identity and presence of person. Symbol is the achievement of real transcending permanent presence of person. Jesus is the sacrament of God means that the man Jesus by being totally authentically human is the total speaking presence of God, Word of God, Word that is God—Word made flesh—the full achievement of image of God. All creation is symbol and sacrament of God which reaches its high point in Jesus, who himself is the mystery of human spirit and human freedom.

In our culture and in our theological tradition, we have spoken of the mystery of faith and have paid lip service to mystery by proclaiming that God is a truth that is greater than the capacity of our reason to understand. We have measured mystery by our own intellectual capacity and have reduced and denied mystery by the comparison. We have made mystery and God a concept. A concept or idea is always our own creation and we end up worshipping our concept of God which is a subtle idolatry.

Sacrament is our involvement in the mystery of all that God really is. Sacrament is a human experience of getting in on the experience of God-being and of being God. It is the real living experience of being truly human. There is nothing "supernatural" or "super human" about it. It is the living human experience of being image of God. Sacrament is the experience of being human; being human is the experience of self-awareness—of being somebody by being "to other." We return again to this affirmation: we are what we are to others, no more, no less, and what we are to others we are to God. Sacrament is the process of being other, the process of people being people to people. This is the human reality which is sacrament.

Significant aspects of this human reality are celebrated and reinforced in seven rituals which we are accustomed to call the seven sacraments. We will identify the human reality that is the sacrament in each instance.

Baptism is the celebration of life at its origin. A child is born a child of love, a child of hope, a child of promise. Parents, family and community celebrate the birth and proclaim their hopes and promise for the child. The child that is born enters the process of being consciously *borne* by the love and care of the community; the child is *named*. Naming is a person-wording, giving an identity. The baptismal ritual is the celebration and affirmation of this human reality which is the sacrament.

The ritually baptized infant is a real named person who cannot yet affirm his or her own identity. This child is really somebody by reason of being borne into the human community and of being what he or she is to all these others who are receiving her or him from God.

In baptism, as in all sacrament, the human sacramental reality is primarily corporate. Baptism is the proclamation and affirmation that the newly named person is born from and borne by the corporate person. It is the affirmation that there is no conflict or adversary tension between the individual and the corporate. The integrity of the individual is not a threat to the corporate; the primacy of the corporate is not a threat to the integrity and rights of the individual. The corporate is the source and maintains and sustains the integrity of the individual. Baptism is the human reality by which every individual is sacrament and symbol of the whole human body that is the Christ. Baptism is the on-going incorporation of the individual into that body in the cosmic creative process. The corporate body zeroes in on this one person not to absorb the person into anonymity, but to call and name the person into real identity in the presence of all other-to-God. Baptism is the creative breathing, spiriting process in which those who are the spirit presence give the spirit to a new other.

Our whole tradition of sacramental theology has been one-sided and too passive. Sacrament is mutuality with God, a giving and a receiving. We have put sacrament into the categories of cause and effect and have made the sacramental reality primarily the effect produced in the individual "recipient." This has confined sacrament primarily to the individual with an official "third party" — Church — "through" its minister, performing the ritual that causes the effect. Our theology has been passive and the practice has been in terms of "receiving" the sacraments. The verbs have been in the passive voice, and the word "sacrament" has been used more as a noun than a verb. The word sacrament like the name of God should be a verb, and if it must be a noun, it should retain the action of the verb and never be plural. "Sacraments" are not things the Church has; sacrament is what the Church does. It is the Church being Church.

The sacrament of baptism is the Church giving the Spirit and the Church receiving the Spirit. The minister of the baptism ritual is sacrament of the giving Church and the person being baptized is sacrament of the receiving Church and the on-going interpresence of giving and receiving the Spirit. This sacramental reality should never be spoken of in the past tense because it is an on-going process in which the person is constantly being born and being borne. It isn't something being done to the person as much as it is what the person is and what it is to be that person. Baptism is constantly receiving total being from God from others and being person by receiving total being. Baptism is a person constantly receiving total freedom from God and from others and being free by receiving it. Baptism is a person constantly receiving human value and dignity in the image of God from God and from others and having the dignity and value of image by receiving it. Baptism is the human reality in which freedom and dignity, real personhood and personal identity are given. There is no real person until dignity and freedom are given and received. It is in this giving and receiving that we are constantly at the point of our origin. This is the point of freedom, the point of all decisions, the point of holiness or sin.

Holiness is openness to receive with the urgency to give what we receive and, in the gospel paradox, to receive by giving. We come into possession of the Spirit when we receive the Spirit from others and give the Spirit to others. Sin is refusal—the affirmation of no need to receive from other—which is a contradiction and denial of self. Sin is the refusal to give what has been received in the false belief that we can possess Spirit and self without giving it.

Baptism is establishment in the total human reality. It is the coming to faith which is our answer to the question "Who are we?" and the awareness that we are what we are to others—no more or no less—and what we are to others, we are to God. All holiness and all sin are in interpersonal relationships. Baptism is this on-going interpersonal process in which we are constantly at our origin and constantly reaching our destiny. All sacrament is baptism; baptism is all sacrament. The others we call sacrament are the celebration of the identifiable phases, stages and functions of this process.

Confirmation is the celebration of the fulfillment of the baptismal promises—the achievement of faith identity. In our time, "affirmation" would be a better name for the celebration in which the faith person is received and acknowledged as belonging to the faith community on the merit of personal faith and decision for personal identity as Christian. Our present ritual and practice are not fully consistent with the sacramental process. First of all, there is nothing sacramental that requires or demands that the minister of the ritual has to be a bishop. The celebration certainly should be significant and memorable, but not exceptional and extraordinary. Being and becoming a Christian is an everyday, and in the right sense of term, ordinary experience. The affirmation of the new adults in the community should be as "ordinary" as the celebration of their birth and should be comfortably within the rhythm and movement of parish life, not subject to or dependent upon the vicissitudes of the bishop's schedule. We must learn to distinguish and separate what is sacramental and what is canonical in the episcopacy, because the church at Podunk is more central to the faith of the people of Podunk than the cathedral. The pastor at Podunk is more central and more involved in the living faith of the people than the bishop.

The celebration of confirmation, or rather affirmation, belongs in the liturgical cycle and in the parish process. In the life process of the community it is a rite of passage, where by invitation of the community, new adults will step forward and proclaim themselves as responsible members of the community to be received and affirmed by the community as really belonging. In our American culture, high school graduation is generally accepted as time for decisions about adult identity and as time for the rituals and celebrations of passage to adulthood. A good suggestion would be that the sacramental celebration of affirmation should take place at Pentecost on the year of high school graduation—not in competition with other ritual functions such as prom—but the celebration should give a faith and spirit dimension to the whole process and make it a rite of passage to Christian adulthood.

In the order of enumeration and in ritual experience, the next sacrament is eucharist. At this point, we come face to face with mystery and confusion. Here we see the crown jewel of the Roman Catholic tradition of faith and at the same time we see the mystery of the presence of God reduced to magic formula and cultic ritual. Eucharist is a prime example of a beautiful tradition of faith in which the poor and the derelict could be comfortable in the presence of God, the proud and powerful could display their arrogance, and the self-righteous could, to their own satisfaction, demonstrate the validity of their claims and their theological conclusions.

We have previously spoken of the common and constant fallacy of making the ritual the sacrament. Today this is preeminently true of the eucharist. It seems that when we started to theologize we stopped believing, because what can be explained can be accepted as fact and really doesn't have to be believed. From the earliest times, but especially in the Refor-mation controversy, we have made the bread and wine the vehicle, the container, or the sign of the presence of the real body and blood of Jesus. Whether this was achieved by tran-substantiation (substance is changed but the accidents remain the same), consubstantiation (substance of the body and blood of Jesus coexists simultaneously under the appearance of bread and wine), impanation (the bread becomes the real body of Christ by the faith of the person receiving at the moment of eating) or by simple faith, the changed bread and wine was, and generally is considered to be the reality of the eucharist. At most and at best, the bread and the wine are *only* ritual. What we call the Mass in our Catholic tradition is not the eucharist. The eucharist is people who are Jesus being raised up in glory in the presence of the Father; the Mass is the celebration of the eucharist.

The primary source of error here is the Greek image of person which we gratuitously accept as primary premise. With this premise, we return to the Upper Room and make Jesus a

Greek speaking to Greeks and develop a whole eucharistic theology on that false premise. In the Upper Room, Jesus is a Hebrew speaking to Hebrews. "Body" and "blood" have an entirely different meaning for the Hebrew than for the Greek or for our peculiar cultural version of the Greek image. For the Hebrew, "bread" and "wine" are symbols, not substances. The verb "to be," "this is," is for the Hebrew a transitive verb.

The word "body" for the Hebrew means "person-present." It is the word for whole real living, existential present person. For the Greek, the word connotes the physical, material element in the human composite of body and soul. For the Hebrew, "blood" likewise is whole person with particular emphasis on life. "Giving" one's blood in Hebrew means literally giving one's life — and it is not even what we would call a figure of speech. Secondly, Jesus uses the demonstrative pronoun "this." The pronoun has to have an antecedent, a prior reference to give it meaning. To what does Jesus refer when he says "*This* is my body" and "*This* is my blood?" The action logic of the Hebrew language would certainly require that the whole action, the "*taking and eating*," and the "*taking and drinking*" would be the antecedent and the reference. It is necessary to be very literal and analytical here because it is the only way to refute a false analysis and unwarranted interpretation of the texts. Returning to a faith hearing, the situation is truly parabolic and we are the disciples to whom the words are being spoken in a real living presence.

Jesus is a Jew speaking to Jews, not a Greek speaking to Greeks. It is a time of parting and of impending doom, but also a paschal moment of faith in the Father's promises; most of all, it is a moment of decision. He has been looking forward to the moment, a high point where He puts it all together and wants us to be with him to get in on His experience. He is not just our representative or agent. He is us and we are him. In taking and offering the bread to us to His Father, he doesn't have to explain to us who are Hebrews what bread means. We know bread is the total gift of God, the gift of self and that bread is the life that it gives and sustains. "Take this bread and eat it" means make my life your life and make your life my life, "for this is my body," means this is (be's) Me; "this is who I am, this is what it means to be Me." People who give and share life and love with each other are my body; they are me.

After supper he takes the cup, the cup of parting, the cup of remembering, the cup for the road, the cup of friendship. For the Jew to remember means more than not to forget. It means to keep it really and existentially present and not to let it become past. This is spoken from a Semitic cultural sense of time in which the present is the permanent establishment of everything prior, the permanent living presence of everything we call past and gone.

Wine is the joy of well-being and like bread, it is for sharing. As bread is really not bread until it is shared and eaten, so wine is really not wine until it is shared and drunk. Life and love exist only in the giving and the sharing. Wine is joy and blood is life. "Take this all of you and drink it, for this is my blood."

In our tradition, rituality has replaced sacramentality in the same cultural process in which we have put the truth in the idea and have made the proposition the object of faith. As we have made the species the sacrament of eucharist, we have made "confession of sin to a duly authorized priest" and his "absolution" the sacrament of forgiveness.

The whole system is a strange mix and confusion of false theological premises about sin and forgiveness: confusion of sacramentality and rituality, confusion of the sacramental and canonical, of gratuitous and false assumption about the creative dynamic and "power" of forgiveness, and arrogant presumptions about the divine institution of the canonical and juridical structure of the Church. In spite of this confusion and poor theology, we have a beautiful faith tradition about the creative healing dynamic of the "confession of sin." We must identify, sort out and separate that which is truly sacramental from the canonical, the juridical, the ritual and the cultural.

The whole matter is about the human reality—experience of sin and forgiveness. The primary source of our confusion is the poor theology of sin and forgiveness. We start traditionally with a definition of sin as a transgression of the law with the result that we make forgiveness a procedure of the law against which the sin was committed. The confusion is compounded by the cultural premise about law as propositions or statements about right and wrong; sin becomes the violation or transgression against the authority that makes the propositions. With such premises we are trapped in legalism and forgiveness becomes a legalistic procedure.

Sin is a transgression against the law of God; the law of God is the real sacramental creative presence of God. The real sacramental creative presence of God is our real living experience in our real living world. The real living world and the people in it are the symbol-sacrament that is the presence of God. Sin is a violation of person and presence. All sin is a violation of interpersonal relationships and a contradiction and denial of image-presence of God.

Our theology of sin has been the logical conclusion of our cultural premises about human person, the nature and process of human decision and about the nature and function of law. In our tradition we have called the human decision the "human act." We have made the human act a product of the person, something that the person does rather than what the person is. We have likewise made each human act a discrete individual entity produced by the interplay of intellect and will for which the performer is responsible and for which the performer merits reward or punishment. In this "merit system," God has become a bookkeeper keeping a production record and ledger of debit and credit constantly current and accurate in the mind of God, but not really open to the person whose account it is. Reward and punishment are credit and debit and "forgiveness" removes the debit without paying the debt. In the economic world, the person is not the money he or she earns or the money he or she owes, but in the moral world, the person is the merit or demerit. Merit or demerit is not something other than or more than the person; merit or demerit is what the person is and has become to others because of the decisions he or she has made.

We have made the forgiveness achieved by the sacrament of confession or penance the altering of the books, changing the record, removal of the debits so that the person stands debt-free and somehow restored to a good credit rating with God. These images are scarcely analogous and are entirely inadequate to explain the creative interpersonal process of presence with God. This interpersonal process of presence with God is our interpersonal process of presence with each other. The process itself is sacrament. Sin is a violation of this presence, a contradiction and denial of identity—a refusal to belong to other and to God. Forgiveness of sin is the restoration and healing of presence and return to favor. Forgiveness is real presence creating love which does not simply remove obstacle or impediment to interpresence but creates the presence itself. There is something greater about forgiveness than the creation of the cosmos itself because it has to undo to uncreate sin, which is not just an absence of good, a nothing or a lack of correspondence with a standard, but sin is a "black hole," a chaos, an un-thing that has to be undone. Forgiveness is a creative un-doing of sin and unmasking of evil. Forgiveness is by the creative power of God who does not make the world out of nothing but out of chaos. Forgiveness brings benign presence out of chaos, affinity out of alienation, creative love out of annihilating fear.

Our sin has brought out the best in God. Given the fact of sin, the first thing about God is not that God is love but that God is love that promises and invites forgiveness. Sacrament is the process in which we are the real presence of God. Penance is the sacrament in which we are the living loving forgiving presence of God for each other. It is the sacrament in which we forgive each other, not the sacrament in which we go to the church to have it done for us. "We believe in the forgiveness of sin" does not mean that we have the ritual and the procedure by which the Church does it for us, but rather that we are a people who are the forgiving power of God and that we take the responsibility to see to it that sin is forgiven.

It takes faith to forgive—not faith that God will forgive us if we are duly repentant—but faith by the offender that the offended will forgive, and faith by the offended that the offender is repentant and wants to be forgiven. Forgiveness is achieved by pure faith, a sacramental process which requires two holy god-like human acts of interpersonal self-creative initiative and response. Forgiveness is not only a restoration. It is a new creation, not a broken relationship repaired but a new presence created. Sin is unpresence, denial and annihilation.

Our language fails again when we speak of the "presence" or even the "existence" of sin, but it is the only way we can affirm its reality. Most of all, there is no question of the reality of the sinner-person, whose contradiction and denial of reality the sin really is, and of the sinned against person, whose dignity and freedom have been denied and contradicted. Forgiveness has to make the contradiction and denial an affirmation, has to make unpresence, real presence and has to make unperson, person. This has to happen in the offender and in the offended. Both the offender and the offended must make a conversion, a self-movement of return to each other. Both offender and offended must take initiative and both must make a response to the initiative of the other. The offended must be open to forgive and the offender must experience the urgency to be forgiven.

The word "conversion" comes from the language of the road. When the traveller "converts" he does not veer off or simply change his direction. He turns around and goes back to where he was and, to be right, he has to go back to where he came from. When a person has sinned so much that he has lost his sense of direction and no longer knows where he came from, he can make no return and cannot be forgiven. This is the unforgivable sin, the hardening of the heart, the sin against the Spirit, which cannot be forgiven because the sinner has come to the point of no return, an irrevocable decision against other, against God. The irrevocability of this decision is not a contradiction of freedom but an affirmation of freedom. Freedom works both ways. Just as there can be a person so good that he can do no evil, a person can become so evil that he can do no good. The paradox of freedom is that freedom can choose to be unfree. The paradox becomes the contradiction that freedom has chosen to be unfree in a permanent irrevocable choice that is hell.

Charity or love is not just the best *motive* for human decisions and for interpersonal relationships; it is the only dynamic of authentic interpersonal relationship. It is not the motive but the movement itself; it is not an extrinsic force but the intrinsic self-initiated movement to the other. Sin has denied and excluded other from self and self from other. Forgiveness is reaffirmation and inclusion. Forgiveness is a covenant process, unconditional and total, the undoing of the offense so that it never even happened.

Our traditional ritual process has made auricular confession one of four conditions for forgiveness. Our traditional process has placed the sin or offense and its malice primarily in the "supernatural" order with ill effects in the "natural" or human order. It has made the sin primarily an offense against God "up there" with consequences "down here" and "confession of sin to a duly authorized priest" a necessary condition for forgiveness.

The four conditions to be fulfilled to qualify for forgiveness were these: 1) contrition, 2) confession, 3) willingness to do penance and 4) purpose of amendment.

The primary fallacy in the requirements is the primacy of the canonical over the truly sacramental, of ritual over sacrament. This is compounded by distinctions and definitions made about contrition itself. The "Act of Contrition" involves a contradiction in terms and an implicit affirmation that there can be forgiveness without conversion. Contrition has been called "perfect" and "imperfect," both in the act and in the quality of the contrition itself. Like Martha, we have been concerned about many things whereas only one thing is necessary. As told in the parable of the prodigal forgiving Father, the sinner must return to God and the child must return to the Father.

Forgiveness is a covenanting process, not a measured, conditional or juridical procedure. A forgiver never says, "I will forgive you 'if.'" A forgiver says, "Here I am. Please come back." It is an unspeakable arrogance for a juridical or canonical authority to presume to establish conditions for the forgiveness of sin and, even worse, for a juridical or canonical authority to presume to have the power to forgive sin. Setting the conditions for forgiveness of sin or presuming the power to forgive sin is clearly beyond the competence of any adversary law but forgiveness is not beyond human competence or power. In fact, forgiveness of sin is the ultimate human responsibility and the ultimate human achievement.

Everything that the resurrection of Jesus is, is within his humanity. Everything that the resurrection is, is in us. We are the body of the resurrection of Jesus and have the resurrection power over sin and death. Given the fact of sin, it can be overcome and done away with, put out of existence and made never even to have happened. This is the resurrection power of forgiveness. This is not an effect of the resurrection nor is it a residual benefit, nor is it an exchange for merit or value. It is a head-on confrontation with evil where it exists, where it has reality—not by an agent or a third party—but by the offended and the offender. It is a situation of great urgency, a unique situation in which both parties take the initiative and in which both parties respond directly and immediately to each other. There is sinner and "sinnee," offender and "offendee." The offender seeks forgiveness; the "offendee" offers pardon. It is not a question of who makes the first move; it is not achieved until each offers and each receives on his or her initiative. The sin offense has violated and destroyed the personal inter-presence that is friendship. Forgiveness recreates and restores a deeper friendship and presence than there was before the offense.

Everything that the Church is, is a response to God to other, to other to God. The Church is the human experience of need and dependence—the faith experience of urgency of total dependence upon other. There is no greater dependence upon other or need of other than there is in the need for forgiveness. The Church is really what is going on between people and God, God and people. The Church is the response to the divine initiative. Specifically, the Church is the human Christ response to the Father. The Christ response is a real existential human experience. It is not vicarious. Jesus is not an agent for us, a third party interceding or intervening in our behalf. In order for Jesus to be really us, he had to be sin and sinner to get in on our experience of sin so that we could get in on his experience of forgiving and of being forgiven. Here we see the full dimension of Spirit. It has to work both ways. Jesus has to become us so that we can become him. Jesus has the experience of forgiving and of being forgiven. The sacrament of forgiveness is the total experience of the forgiveness process. Forgiveness is not instant. It is a process in interpersonal relationship. It is not forgiveness until it is total. Although it does not need a lot of time, it does need a lot of movement. It needs complete change of direction. The openness and willing-ness on the part of the "offendee" is a movement and an open invitation to the offender to return to the interpresense that is friendship. The offender is received and welcomed, not "as if" there had been no offense but the offense is removed and done away with. It is made never to have happened at all. The willingness and urgency to forgive is itself a new level of the presence that love is and the desire and urgency to be forgiven is not simply restoration, but a new level and new depth of friendship.

Forgiving and being forgiven are always a new experience, always a sacramental first time, always something unique and something that never happened before. Conversion and forgiveness are always new and alive; reversion to sin is always old and a return to death.

While forgiving is always a new and creative experience, it really does make a lot of sense. It is an experience in the mastery of one's own destiny. There is no neutral alternative to sin. Sin cannot be tolerated and remain the same. Tolerated and unforgiven, sin takes on new dimension of evil simply by being tolerated and unforgiven. The experiential dimension of toleration and unforgiveness is resentment, bearing a grudge, alienation, suspicion, erosion and deterioration of the total impersonal situation and relationship. Resentment is a slow burn, an ulcer maker that makes the "burnee" miserable by choice and gives the offender a power and a control over one's life.

It is not a virtue not to be offended. It is a sin to take offense when there is none. It is amoral or insensitive not to be offended when real offense is given. Tolerance is a virtue. Tolerance does not excuse sin but tolerance will excuse behavior that inadvertently gives offense. Tolerance does not assign motives. Tolerance will reserve judgment and will distinguish between offense and mistake.

Popular American cultural premises and attitudes are not a friendly environment for the gospel demands for forgiveness. Peter's question to Jesus in Matthew 18/21, "How often must I forgive my brother, seven times?" would get quite a different answer in the American cultural setting. Rambo Americans would say "Never! Forgiveness is weakness; reprisal is strength and justice is getting even." We are political, social and moral "conservatives" who think that our written (positive) laws account for all morality. In our Western system, the written laws—including the laws of the Church—prescribe and require only a minimum. Forgiveness is not included in that minimum requirement. Forgiveness remains a kind of an option for heroes only. Forgiveness is an ordinary requirement for the gospel way of life. Forgiveness is expected of everybody in the Christian community and becomes the unique characteristic that sets the people of the Kingdom of God above and apart from the people of the world.

It is interesting to note that the classic Greek and Latin languages did not have a word for "forgive" or "forgiveness." The Apostolic Hebrew Christian community gave us their version of the Lord's prayer something close to the words of the instruction of Jesus himself. The earliest Greek Christian community did not have the word for "forgive us our sins." It seems the best they could do was the Greek equivalent of the familiar Latin "Dimitte nobis debita nostra," a linguistic contrivance, meaning "dismiss, or write-off our debts." In our English version, we at least have the word "forgive." We would do much better to say "forgive us our sins," than to say the approved "forgive us our debts, or trespasses" or whatever.

We don't like to multiply distinctions or split hairs but do we "forgive sin," "forgive the sinner" or both? What is the object of forgiveness? The object of forgiveness is both sin and sinner but sin and sinner are really one. Sin is a failure; the sinner is a failed person. The evil of sin is "in" the person and "in" the person's interrelationship with other. The sin is a failure to be or to do and the reality of the sin is that the sinner really isn't the person he or she really should be.

At this point, the pedants and the sophists would enter into their inane discussion of the objectivity and subjectivity of sin. Forgiveness confronts the reality of sin. Forgiveness meets real sin head-on and annihilates it, destroys it to the point that it never even existed. Forgiveness is the ultimate and only answer to God.

A deep dimension of the evil of our time is that we have lost our consciousness and awareness of personal sin. Perhaps a deeper dimension of the evil of our time is that we have never had an awareness of the corporate dimension of sin. Corporate sin is much more than the accumulation of the sins of the individuals of the community. Corporate sin is more than simple failure which leaves things undone; corporate sin is evil at work. It is the acceptance and endorsement of the false prophet. The failure of the Northern Kingdom of Israel was the corporate sin condemned by the prophets Amos and Osee. The failure of Judah was the corporate sin condemned by Jeremiah. The failure of the Jews to accept the Christ was the corporate sin of the people that rejected him and the continuing failure of Christianity is the corporate sin of the people to whom the gospel has been preached.

Corporate sin as personal sin can be undone only by conversion and forgiveness. In every human situation of urgent decision, there are true prophets and false prophets. Sin is evil done. Evil done is evil present. Confrontation with evil done or being done is unavoidable and the confrontation is prophetic. False prophets deny the evil they can't ignore, ignore the evil they can't deny and always find believers who want to be told "Everything is all right. We never had it so good. Our troubles will go away." The true prophet has to say, "Our troubles are own making. We have failed as a people and as a people we must repent and convert." The prophet proclaims the corporate sin and guilt and calls for a corporate repentance. We must confront the evil that threatens us or it will destroy us. We must confront evil in ourselves, convert from it, confront evil in others and be willing to forgive it out of existence. If evil doers do not and cannot convert, their sin cannot be forgiven. This is the sin against the Spirit. It is unforgivable because the sinner's hardened heart is irrevocably set against God and other.

Because the hardened heart irrevocably excludes God, the person of the hardened heart irrevocably excludes himself from the community of the people of God. Sacrament includes all who are open to God to other. Matrimony is the sacrament of creative openness to other. Marriage is the achievement of an indissoluble, exclusive permanent commitment of a man and a woman to be husband and wife to each other until death. The persons are the marriage, not the ritual or the record. We are inclined to limit the sacramental reality to that which husband and wife are to each other in a kind of a one way relationship to the rest of society. The rest of society is really sacramentally involved in every marriage. The support, sustenance and reinforcement of marriage is a corporate sacramental function and responsibility of human society. It belongs to and is an extension of the societal witnessing required in the ceremonial proclamation of the marriage commitment. We emphasize the requirement for the canonical and civil validity of the proclamation on the part of the husband and wife and remain quite unaware of the commnity responsibility to receive, honor, support and protect the marriage promises.

Human marriage is rooted in creation itself, not as a law imposed extrinsically, but it is itself the creative power and presence of God. As God cannot annhilate or uncreate anything he has made, so marriage is indissoluble. Marriage is the law of God's love and imposes the requirements of God's love in any and all human interpersonal relationships. The law of love can be denied and broken in marriage as in any other human situation. The promise can be broken and the love union dissolved by failure and denial to the point that it no longer exists. Such failure is sinful but it is real. The broken promise and failed commitment are sinful and broken even to the point that it is irreparable and it becomes part of the sin of the world. The sin is a failed marriage. A failed marriage is more than a failed project or a simple broken promise. A failed marriage is the annihilation and destruction of an interpresence with God; it is sin. In the situation, the sin cannot be denied, but the question must be, is it an unforgiveable sin? It is not. The only unforgivable sin is the ultimate sin, the sin against the Spirit, the hardening of the heart that cannot convert and turn back to God. A failed marriage no longer exists but the persons who have been the marriage continue to exist, and given forgiveness, their sin no longer exists and they are restored to full freedom before God and his people. This includes freedom to marry. The previous marriage no longer exists. It has been denied and destroyed by the failure of the persons who are the marriage. Marriage is a human reality, under the same law of failure and death as everything else that is human, but under the same responsibilty to "take and keep" as all the rest of human life. Failure in marriage is part of the sinful human condition.

A broken promise is not only no longer a promise, it is a nothing. It is a contradiction and a denial. A broken and failed marriage is not just something that doesn't exist anymore, it is a human failure that must be confronted and overcome. We tend to evaluate and judge the social and moral situation of marriage and divorce by statistics and numbers which indicate an alarming divorce rate. This rate is determined by registrar's records which presume that every unit recorded is a marriage in the first place. Our greatest problem is not the rate of divorce, but the rate of non-marriage in the first place, which appears on the record as a real marriage and becomes a divorce statistic.

In our culture, we are woefully unaware of the dynamic of growth and decay in the process of the human spirit in the marriage experience. We romantically consider the love of courtship the highest love and cynically project that marriage itself is inevitably a dull drudgery doomed to decline. Failure in marriage is failure in faith. Authentic marriage requires faith. Faith in marriage is reasonable expectation of husband and wife from each other and an awareness of the human effort required to sustain the faith. It is often said that it would be easier and better if people knew the future. If we knew the future, there would be no room for faith, the dimension of promise would be reduced and eventually there would be nothing to believe in.

More marriages fail because people expect too little from marriage than that they expect too much. To believe is to have expectations. To believe in marriage is to have expectations from marriage. Marriage is persons united with mutual expectations, believing in each other, being willing to believe in and to be believed in. This faith is a mutual understanding and awareness that accepts reasonable expectations and avoids unreasonable demands. An authentic marriage is a creative interpresence, the sacramental image of the creative interpresence of God and the universe.

All sacrament is interpresence of God and his people in the person of the Christ. The dynamic of interpresence is care and concern for the salvation, the well being of the whole community of believers in every situation of their human existence. The specific need of the sick and dying for the care and concern of others is met in the sacrament of Extreme Unction, the anointing of the sick.

In the Christian origin, anointing with oil was part of the care for the sick. Oil was used for healing and comfort and it was a natural human process from which a ritual anointing developed. As the sacramental ritual developed, anointing itself was not intended to be the healing function but a sacramental sign of the healing presence of the Church, the Christian community.

From the earliest times, there have been those accepted and designated by the community for this particular ecclesial function of visiting the sick. There is today in the Church, a welcome return of the function to the general body of the faithful in our care for the sick as the proper function of the permanent deacon and the designated visitors.

We should become aware that our practice of visiting the sick in hospitals and in health care facilities is the sacramental reality. In practice, our health care facilities are a mixed blessing.

In many instances, they are commercial. In everyday structures and functions of society, we have no room or time for the care of the sick and think that we are adequately caring for them by isolating them into professional medicial units with, at times, impersonal care.

In our compulsion to categorize all the aspects of our human behavior, we tend to violate the organic unity of the human spirit. We speak of spiritual and corporal works of mercy as a specific dimension of Christian behavior that is very good but less than sacramental because they are not performed by a ritually designated person. The care and nuturing of the human person is the ongoing creative work of the Spirit.

Traditionally, the sacrament of extreme unction was reserved for those who were "in danger of death" from their particular illness. Contemporary practice very properly extends the sacrament to all who are seriously sick. It would be most proper to look to the gospel for the "institution" of the sacrament and to find Jesus moved to compassion speaking his healing with a kind word and a saving touch. The same Spirit is alive and the same Christ finds his healing presence where believers moved with compassion assist their sick and bring the gifts of their healing presence. This is the full dimension of the sacrament.

Hurting people of our time are finding the healing presence of the Spirit in the dynamic of the group. Such groups are broadly identified as "self help" groups who meet to support and sustain each other in their suffering from addiction or disease. The rituals that develop in the creative dynamic of such groups are a prime example of the development of sacramental ritual in authentic human experience.

We would do well to come aware that every sacrament is the giving of the Spirit. In our Christian tradition, healing has always been a primary function of the Spirit Presence. The giving of the Spirit to the sick is the same Spirit and the same giving as we hear in "receive my Spirit...whose sins you shall forgive they are forgiven," whose infirmities you heal, they are healed. (John 20-22)

Every culture is a functioning value system. Cultural premises are ultimately value judgments that are held in common by the people who are the culture. In the cultural process, structures and institutions are established to maintain, sustain and proclaim the cultural values. Every culture, in one way or another, will divide its values into the sacred and the profane, even to the point, as in our contemporary secular culture, of holding sacred the right to deny that there is anything sacred.

The culture is the environment for the Church. The Church originated out of the Hebrew religious tradition in the Greek cultural context. The early Christian community inherited a sense of the sacred from this compound origin, a sense of the "secret" from the circumstances of its earlier gatherings under persecutions, and a sense of joyful proclamation from the freedom of better days. In the cultural process, there came to be accepted ways to make the affirmations of the sacred and to designate persons to be keepers and proclaimers of the sacred.

In practice, a person is a cleric before the reception of orders. Being a cleric is a canonical not a sacramental state. Today, a candidate for orders is canonically accepted and proclaimed by the reception of tonsure. Tonsure is admission to the clergical state signified by the cutting or shaving of the hair from the head of the person. (See chapter on Morality.)

Ordination is not the authorization or empowerment of a person, but the affirmation of identity and role of ministry. The authentic image of the priesthood should not be that of privileged persons somehow raised above the status of ordinary people. The image of priesthood should be an image that incorporates and proclaims the dignity and the honor of the whole people. The priest is not a person who performs sacramental functions for the laity, but a person who is given and holds the dignity and privilege of what the people are called to be. Priests can be no more and no better than the people for whom he or she is priest. The holiness and function of the priesthood does not come from God through the priest to the people, but rather, from God through the people to the priest. The sacramental source for the priesthood is the baptized people of God with whom there is "neither Jew nor Greek. There can be neither slave nor freeman. There can be neither male nor female, for you are all one in Christ Jesus." (Galatians 3/28) The priest is not a performer or doer of the sacraments, but one who is sacrament of the people for whom he or she is priest in the presence of God. Sexual identity or social status can exclude no person from priesthood anymore than it could exclude a person from peoplehood.

The sacrament of orders is essentially the whole community process of selecting, designating and proclaiming persons as ministers to the worshipping community and keepers and proclaimers of the sacred. Although today we make a clear distinction saying that only priesthood and episcopacy are Holy Orders, the sacrament is broadly comprised of a series of minor orders.

The minor orders in their origin were a ministry of service to the worshipping community: lector, the reader of the scriptures; the janitor, the watchman and keeper of the door; the exorcist, the expeller of evil spirits; and the acolyte, the light bearer, whose duties included the preparation of the altar and gifts for the liturgy.

In our time, there is the restoration of the order of deaconate as a ministry of service but we regret that it has too often becomes an extension and expansion of clerical status and privilege. The presbyterate or priesthood had a specifically cultic development as a role of leaership in the liturgical worship. Today the identity of the designated person is commonly known as the "priest." The episcopacy is universally accepted as being sacramental major orders. In its origin, the emphasis of episcopacy was on the priesthood. Today, the image of the episcopacy seems to be primarily a juridical and canonical function rather than a ministry of orders. (See chapter on "Church" for further developent of the priesthood, episcopacy and papacy.)

There is nothing scriptural, sacramental or theological that would require celibacy as a condition for the reception of orders. It is a contradiction to assume that the sacrament of matrimony is an impediment to the function of the sacrament of orders. There perhaps was a historical moment when the committed celibate state was accepted as a higher and more perfect way of life for those who freely chose it. Given the social acceptability of the celibate state, it would have been reasonable to expect the cleric to measure up to that accepted standard. In this way, celibacy for the cleric came to be accepted and imposed as a discipline of the Church. It was and remains a Church discipline, not a divine institution. As a discipline, it can be justified only by its meaning and power to witness the gospel way of life. (See chapter on Christology.)

In the contemporary Christian community, the unmarried state does not have that meaning nor does it give such witness in our time. Whatever celibacy is, it should not exclude a marriage. Every person must somehow marry because marriage achieves a personal fulfillent by a personal commitment to other. The essence of marriage is the achevement of personal union with God. The celibate must make this same high level marriage commitment of service to other in a specific ministry of the gospel way of life.

There is nothing scriptural, sacramental or theological to exclude women from the sacrament of orders. To exclude women from ordination is an implication that women are less baptized or poorer believers and doers of the Word than men. Social processes and the everyday experience of our times proclaim that women are true believers and initiators of the faith process. They are proficient and competent in every aspect of social service and teaching of the gospel way of life.

Christian sacrament is individual and corporate involvement and working interpresence with God. Sacrament is rooted in faith, which is the living awareness of presence, not just the acceptance of doctrine or rational conclusion. Sacramental faith is the vision of the working presence of God in the community of believers. This loving faith is proclaimed and reinforced in the celebration of the sacramental ritual.

The Second Vatican Council is not simply an isolated event in the recent history of the Church, it is really a continuing event of sacramental renewal and change which is the work of the Spirit. Marvelous things have happened and are happening in the Church in our time that are a revival of the Spirit, a new Pentecost, a new and deepening awareness of the spirit dimension of the resurrection. The Church has become aware that the resurrection and the coming of the Spirit are an ongoing event. The Church itself is that event and believers in the spirit of the Risen One have reason and cause for celebration. A generation of liturgical renewal that was primarily focused on ritual is becoming sacramental. There is the urgency for quality ritual performance because the sacramental celebration requires it. People are no longer just "going to church," they are coming to celebrate the eucharist. The laity are coming into what is properly their own, the awareness of the dignity and privilege of their status as committed baptized persons. More is expected of the cleric and ordained minister; clerical privilege and immunity is eroding and no longer gratuitously accepted as a divine institution. All sacrament is the celebration of belonging. To belong to God, to be good enough for God, to be son and daughter of God, to enter into a covenant of total mutuality with God by our own choice is certainly cause for celebration. We are coming into our own. Knowing who we are to God and the immediacy and urgency of God's presence in us and to us is faith. Faith requires celebration.

13
MORALITY

THE RESPONSIBILITY OF BEING HUMAN

"FOR THIS LAW THAT I ENJOIN ON YOU TODAY is not beyond your strength or beyond your reach. It is not in heaven, so that you need to wonder who will go up to heaven for us and bring it down to us, so that we may hear it and keep it. No, the Word is very near to you, it is in your mouth and in your heart for your observance." (Deuteronomy 30/11-14.)

Law doesn't just tell us what to do, it gives us good things to be free about—good things to do. The physical law of the conservation of energy at the root of a dynamic universe sets the tone and pattern for the cosmic thrust of return to God for which human freedom is the leading edge. Human freedom is moral power of creativity. Morality is not a passive conformity to an extrinsic standard or model, but it is a unique power of human self-creativity. Morality is not goodness or authenticity accorded to a human decision, but it is the intrinsic power of a human decision to authenticate a person in the image of God. Morality is the ultimate creative dynamic of the human spirit; it is the self-movement of the return to God.

Law is the source of morality. Law is the ongoing creative power and presence of God. Freedom is the human response to the creative presence. Freedom is mysteriously totally dependent upon the continuing creative presence of God and, at the same time, self-initiated in the very image of the creator upon whom it is dependent. Our total dependence on God is not a limitation, but it is itself a response to a sustaining presence that saves us from the contradiction of being without God. Freedom is at the same time a totally dependent response and a self-initiated movement in the experience of being human.

It is human to reflect on the experience of being human. From the first movement of human consciousness, human beings have marvelled and wondered at what it means to be human. From the beginning, what it means to be human has been a question and a search for the vision of all that it means to be human and how to achieve the vision. This has been the constant human endeavor. The human person in a unique way is the leading edge of the cosmic urgency to become something that is not yet. The uniqueness of the human experience is a sense of urgency and self-initiative to become somebody that is not yet, to be free standing and autonomous. This unique human experience is the moral experience. Morality is the achievement of authentic humanity.

It is authentically human to be creative in the image of the Creator. Self-creativity is the highest level of human creativity and all human creativity is somehow self-creativity. The human creation is always in the image of the human creator as God's creation is always in the divine image. Morality is the unique experience of becoming human by self-creativity. Part of the experience of being human is to reflect on the experience itself. We search deeper and deeper into our past and present experience of being human in our sciences of anthropology, archaeology and history; we find that being human is never static. This search discovers that people will either strive to become somebody and something that they are not yet and achieve it or, if they settle for a status quo, they will deteriorate and die out.

The human experience of vision and achievement or loss of vision and deterioration is the moral experience. While the moral experience is self-initiated, it is a response to the source of the vision. The source of the vision is something or someone other than and other to the person who has the vision. The search for and the discovery of such a source is the religious experience. The acceptance of such a source is religious faith; the source itself becomes the god of the believer. The religious experience is a moral experience.

This confrontation with mystery, the awareness that there is something bigger than we are is a common and universal human experience. There is even the experience that there is something about us that is bigger than we are, and the question "Who am I?" and "Who are we?" are themselves a confrontation with mystery, the sense of the presence of some other "out there, right here" with a sense of urgency to seek, find, know and become involved with that other. This is the religious experience common to all people, but unique in every person and in every cultural group.

The religious experience is the subject matter for theology; the religious experience specifically as a study of human behavior is the subject matter for ethics, moral philosophy and moral theology. The religious experience itself is a search and the study of the experience becomes a search of a search. It is a search for and an investigation of sources, both for the law and human behavior in response to the law. Ethics or moral philosophy is the study of human reason as itself being both the source and the vision, while moral theology is based on the premise that the vision itself is a response to the totally other who is God.

Morality is the human participation in the expanding universe which is a process of creative response which is much more than a series of cause and effect relationships. We tend to have such faith in the adequacy of our ontological categories that we think everything can be explained in terms of cause and effect. We have even attempted to establish and prove the existence of God by assuming that creation is a cause-effect phenomenon in which there cannot be an infinite series of cause and effect. The argument is in itself a contradiction in terms. In pursuing a series of cause and effect back to the original cause, one would have to arrive at some point at the uncaused cause who would be God. Our logic arrives at God as first cause or uncaused cause but really does not arrive at the real God, who is Father, creator of heaven and earth.

It is an arrogant and gratuitous assumption to accept the adequacy of the category of cause and effect to explain everything and anything, including creation. An effect is always somehow less than the cause. By simple cause and effect, the cosmos would be caught in the law of diminishing returns with each effect being somewhat less than its cause. Quite the opposite is true. The universe, with humankind at its leading edge, is an expanding universe under the law of "increase and multiply." Every creature is invested with a dynamic of self-creativity and self-determination that is more than simple causality. If it were simple causality, the effect would be greater than its cause. The universe is expanding by an intrinsic dynamic of self-creativity. Being human and human being is the leading edge of the cosmic process.

Each atom does its own "atoming," each tree does its own "treeing" and each person does his or her own "personing." God dignifies every creature by removing his/her necessity as far as possible and puts every creature on its own. Every creature not only shares the creative word and creative power, but every creature is itself a creative presence of the word "increase and multiply."

The creative power and presence that all things are is the law; the specific human creative power and presence to make self and the world is morality. Morality is the creative dynamic of human freedom by which good decisions are creative and bad decisions are annihilative. Good decisions "increase and multiply"; bad decisions "decrease and destroy."

There is an element of self-achievement and self-movement at every level of creation from the whirling particles of the atom to the self-movement of human freedom. The apparent determined response of the physical laws is in harmony with the law that is human freedom and is not a contradiction of freedom. Our freedom power to use these laws is itself within the compatibility and harmony of the entire creative process. In the organic structure of the cosmic response to God's creative presence, human freedom is the point at which the universe meets God and God meets the universe, most closely and most intimately. This meeting is morality.

A common and simple question in seeking the purpose of a thing is to ask "What is it for; what is it good for?" The question is simple and comprehensive and serves well in seeking the human purpose. "What is he or she for; what is he or she good for?" Being human is good for being happy. All the commandments put into two words would be "Be happy." Happiness is not the reward for being good, it is simply good human being.

The primary and unique characteristic of human being or being human is introspective self-awareness. The experience of being human is itself a search into the meaning and purpose of being human. This human search into meaning and purpose is always made with a sense of urgency. There is urgency in the response of every creature to its environment. There is the urgency of the seed to sprout, of the plant to grow, to blossom and to bear fruit. There is the urgency of the egg to hatch, of the fledgling to fly and in its own turn to mate, nest and hatch its own brood. Urgency to be and to do what it has been made to do is the common experience of every creature from the lowest to the highest, from the atom to the human spirit. The human experience of urgency is more than a unique human introspective self-awareness. The unique human experience is the experience of introspective self-awareness which is a self-initiated self-image of the person that one is at the moment. But beyond that, there is a vision of what that person can become and a sense of urgency to become that person. The sense of urgency, the sense of inner movement toward a decision to do what one ought to do is the unique human experience which is conscience, which is itself the ongoing moral experience of being human.

In God's world, all creatures are ordered in their own way to achieve the end or purpose for which they have been created. Morality is this creative ordering for those created in his image.

Morality is good human being and it is not a simple platitude to say that only good people can be happy. To be good is to be truly happy and to be truly happy is to be good.

Our common experience of what we are pleased to call conscience is happiness or unhappiness according to the decisions that we make. Good decisions make us happy; bad decisions make us unhappy. The awareness of the immediacy of happiness or unhappiness in our decisions is at the root of the urgency of the decisions.

In our moral tradition, we have set up a merit system of "*quid pro quo*" in which we receive or acquire a credit or debit according to the character and quality of decisions we make. The merit or the debit in this system is not the decision or the person but a third entity somehow added to the person. Happiness or unhappiness of moral decision is the very identity of the person making the decision. It is who the person is for the decision that has been made. Law is the continuing creative presence of God inviting us to make ourselves happy by our own choice of identity. Morality is the creative dynamic of our interpresence with God.

The Law of God is the revealing presence of God. The law is God present revealing who he is by revealing who we are in his image. Law and revelation are a continuing creative presence, a constant presence—constant and continuing in the changing circumstances and situation of every moment. Situations change but the transcending presence of God is constant and every situation and every human experience is in its own way a revelation of God.

Much of the discussion and controversy about morality in our time has centered about "situation ethics." Traditionalists call situation ethics "relativism" and deny its validity because it implies a denial of any moral absolutes. In the controversy, the absolutists gratuitously assume the premise of the adequacy of the categories of the absolute and relative, with the same conclusion that the only establishment of moral certitude and real moral criteria is on the premise of moral absolutes. It is not a matter of rejecting the adequacy of moral absolutes, but of questioning the very validity of moral absolutes.

The ultimate criterion of morality, of the authenticity of human behavior, is not an ontological category, but human nature and human being. That which is authentically human is moral and that which contradicts or denies being human is immoral. In this search, we do not look for absolutes, but for constants. A constant is more than an absolute. An absolute is an abstraction about an abstraction. A constant is an existential living reality. The moral constant is what things should and ought to be in any and every situation and circumstance. It is not a matter of changing situations that have changing laws, but a matter of a transcending constant law governing changing situations. The point is that the situation itself reveals the law that governs it. The situation does not determine the law; it simply reveals the law.

A situation ethic is consonant with the theology of revelation. Creation is God speaking. God words his universe and everything in it. The universe itself is the speaking presence of God; God does not speak to his universe from outer space or from some point outside of the universe. In a growing and expanding universe, the speaking presence of God grows and expands with the universe. Believers are persons who can read and hear God's speaking presence wherever and whenever he speaks; believers always hear a present speaking. Believers know that God has spoken in times past, but that his word is always the word of the present moment spoken with the urgency of the present moment in which it is believed. The word is being spoken to a believer at the very moment of believing.

The Word made flesh is the ultimate in situation ethics. All of Scripture is a moral revelation spoken to believers in every instance as the Word of God for a specific human situation. God's speaking presence is for every changing moment spoken specifically to the situation of the moment in such a way that the very situation itself is the revealing speaking presence. God reveals himself to the world in a way in which the world itself is the revealing presence.

Morality is traditionally defined as the conformity of the human act or human behavior to accepted standards for human acting. Morality thus becomes identified as traditional, Christian, modern or "new" according to the source or authority from which the standards are derived and promulgated. The first step in presenting a credible morality is to establish a credible authority. Just what it is that constitutes a valid moral authority is the basic moral issue. Moral authority is the source of law and just what constitutes valid authority and just what is the proper function of law is the ongoing moral question.

Law is more than a proposition or statement of good to be done and evil to be avoided. Law is the sacrament of the creative presence of God. Law is God present creating. Human conscience is the moral experience of urgency of response to the creative presence which is law. Human conscience is the moral experience of urgency to be the person we know we should be and the law of God is the continuing creative presence of God giving us the vision of the person we should be and the experience of urgency to become that person. It goes so far as to give an experience of the joy of accomplishment for achieving the vision and the sadness of remorse for failure. In the moral experience that is conscience, we are all our own law-givers.

Conscience is the experience of the urgency of self-creativity which is the self-creative dynamic of the human personality in the corporate and the individual. As the individual is in every instance of moral decision his or her own lawgiver, so the corporate person, the human community on every level is its own lawgiver. The right, the competence and the power to give law, to "make" laws, is authority. There are many opinions and theories about the constitution and nature of authority or source of law for the human community. Just as theories and opinions about the nature of individual personality will vary from system to system, so there will be different theories about the source and competence of the corporate or public lawgiver or law-maker. The point to be made is that just as there is in every individual person the dimension of no neutrality, so it is with the corporate person. The contemporary issue is not primarily a question of theory about the constitution of government and political structure, but a question about the reality of the corporate personality and corporate responsibility. Just as individual persons will prosper or fail according to their response to individual conscience, so will corporate persons, nations and societies, prosper or fail according to the response to corporate conscience. All of Scripture affirms a primacy of the corporate personality and corporate conscience. The "Adam and Eve" story of human origin is a moral affirmation of corporate conscience and corporate responsibility. All of Scripture speaks of the corporate moral experience of the people of God.

The story that tells the giving of the ten commandments is a statement about the corporate conscience of the people of God. The ten commandments are a corporate conscience statement of that person talking to himself. The ten commandments are the second person affirmation and response to the first person affirmation of the creative presence "I am the Lord thy God." The whole cultural process is the process of a corporate personality. Ancient cultures seemed to be aware of this when they promulgated their laws in the second person imperative, as the ten commandments came to us in the Scriptures. The moral law is the extension of the "you are" which is itself the creative word, and the ten commandments as all of Scripture is the spoken faith response of the believer. In the ten commandments, we have in ten bold strokes a dramatic self-portrait of a person covenanted with God, the person given to and belonging to God. Morality is human freedom at work, keeping the law of God. "To keep" the law does not mean simple conformity to the law, but "to keep" is a creative word first spoken when God gave Adam and Eve the garden which is the image of total human responsibility and tells them "to take it and keep it." Morality is human freedom at work keeping the laws and putting the law to work to make us the persons we are called to be in the presence of God. The presence of other persons is the presence of God.

Morality is not an abstraction about human behavior, but it is the living reality of interpersonal presence and relationships. Morality is what is going on between people on all levels and in every dimension of being human. Morality is the interpresence of persons in a common possession of the Spirit that is God. Morality is confrontation with total reality, a meeting with the entire universe. This meeting is on all levels of human experience and touches and involves the total reality and all things that bring people into relationship with each other. The Genesis story of creation is primarily a moral affirmation. "Take it and keep it," is an affirmation of moral responsibility for the universe as an environment for creating and maintaining interpersonal relationships in the "image of God" in which he created them. As God is God for others, person made in his image is person for others. Person for self is the same contradiction as God for self.

As the total otherness of God is the establishment of the integrity of individual human personality, the self-creativity of human freedom is the dynamic of moral decision in the experience of being person for other.

There is mystery in being moral. There is something about being human that is bigger than we are. A believer can be more human than a pure logician. The ethics of logic can be convincing; the morality of faith is persuasive. The individual decision made in favor of the group establishes the integrity of the individual. It is only by authentically entering the mystery of self that decision for interpersonal relating can be met. By entering the mystery of self, the mystery of other is met and corporate connection begins to happen.

There must be quality and integrity in the "I" of "I love" in which to ground authentic interpersonal relationship. Fear and compulsion distort the integrity of self and surrender ownership in a way that gives power to other, which becomes a power over others that violates the true corporate. This is a real problem in many social relationships. There are many things that erode the integrity of the "I" in "I am." Persons give away their "I" for addiction or surrender to a multitude of false others as evidence in recovering alcoholics to recovering Catholics. Surrender to authoritarianism breeds self-hatred. Authoritarianism on any level denies and robs persons of the integrity of their "I."

Interpersonally, perhaps, we are at a kind of an adolescent stage in our society. There is on one side, the phenomenon of mass conformity to fads or movements and persuasion by image politically or socially without critical judgment. It is a great opportunity for the false prophet who is believed when we are told that all is well, there have never been better times. People, who believe the false prophets, are adolescents committed to get their share with no awareness of the exclusion of others in the process. This violent adolescent primacy of the individual violates the integrity of the individual and destroys the grounding for the true corporate.

If we dare to move beyond mass conformity to the integrity of the individual, we will find and draw from others their own deeper integrity. Like will find like, move toward and bond with other of the same kind in a creative interpersonal relationship which is morality.

Morality is the dynamic of a healthy tension working mutually from the individual to the corporate and from the corporate to the individual. This creates and sustains a healthy environment in which we "take and keep" the world as our human moral responsibility.

There are two levels of human response to God, the individual and the corporate. On each level, the unique characteristic of human response is that the response is self-initiated decision for individual or corporate identity. The self-initiation of the response is that which makes us human and in the image of God with moral responsibility.

Establishing a moral authority or source of law is a cultural and sociological process. Archaeology, history and sociology witness the rise and fall of peoples and nations and that the dynamic of growth or decline is the corporate conscience. The image a people have of themselves will be and become the reality that the people are. The corporate experience and vision of an ideal becomes a moral urgency and the cultural striving of a people to achieve the ideal, whereas the loss of vision and ideal erodes the moral urgency and inevitably leads to the decline and fall of the people.

All law is a creative force. The ultimate source of all law is the conscience of the people who are governed by the law, and the law will fail at its very source when the conscience of the people dies. Peoples and nations have died with good laws "on the books." A system or structure of law has to remain rooted and alive in the corporate conscience of a people in order to create and sustain the authentic moral identity of a people.

Heroes and myths in a culture are primarily moral affirmations and expectations of the conscience of a people. Heroes and myths can live on in the symbol and in the art of a people even when they die in the flesh. People fail their heroes and myths by failing to become and to be the people imaged in them.

Christianity is a moral revelation in the corporate creative human process. Christianity does not begin with the historic birth of the Christ. The hymn to the first-born in Paul's letter to the Colossians 1/15-20 is the presentation of the Christian moral image.

> He is the image of the unseen God,
> the firstborn of all creation,
> for in him were created things
> in heaven and on earth:
> everything visible and everything invisible,
> thrones, ruling forces, sovereignties, powers—
> all things were created through him and for him.
> He exists before all things
> and in him all things hold together,
> and he is the Head of the Body,
> that is, the Church.
> He is the Beginning,
> the firstborn from the dead,
> so that he should be supreme in every way;
> because God wanted all fullness to be found in him
> and through him to reconcile all things to him...

Paul's hymn to the firstborn is an echo of the song of the psalmist about the glory of being human when he exclaims:

> You have made them a little less than God,
> you have crowned them with glory and beauty,
> put them in charge of all the works of your hands
> and put all things at their feet. (Psalms 8/5-6)

A true human conscience is a moral sense, an awareness of the glory and the dignity of being human with a sense of urgency to achieve the glorious image in which we have been created. The great moral failure of traditional Christianity is a failure in faith. Faith is the answer to the question "Who are we, what does it mean to be human?" It is this failure in faith that has made our real moral heroes contrived exceptions to the rule. The glorious human achievement of the faith of Mary has been lost in the contrivance of our false image of her being "tainted nature's solitary boast" in the Immaculate Conception. She becomes the heroine figure only by being the exception to the rule.

A dogmatic theology that makes Jesus more and better than human by contriving the doctrine of hypostatic union is a denial of "Word made flesh." Our cultural image of being human is a moral disaster and we have had to make our "heroes" more and better than human to make them credible. All our hero saints are honored more for being miraculous exceptions than for being the affirmation of the rule of being human. We have implicitly denied the glory and wonder of being human by excluding being "only human" from our definition of "miracle" as being beyond and above being human. Humanity is the ultimate miracle, the glory of being human is God's greatest work and Christian morality is the greatest human achievement.

It is the purpose and function of law to make this miracle happen. Law is God's continuing creative presence. Obedience to the law is to have and to accept the vision that the law presents and to experience the urgency to achieve it. It is the function of authority to be source of vision and credibly to present the vision and the promise. This is achieved primarily by being a living promising presence of what a person can be and become in what we are pleased to call "good example." Our language "good example, role model" is really not adequate; such a person is a real immediate creative presence. Such a person is primary law, authority at work, and sacrament of the creative presence of God. In this way, the resurrection, the risen one is primarily a most urgent moral revelation. The resurrection is not just a conceptual vision, but a living presence. He is "raised up" to our faith and we "raise him up" by accepting the vision with the urgency to become the person that he is. He gives his Spirit and in receiving his Spirit we become the person he is and live his life. This life is not just a life modeled after his, but his very own life. Living this life and being this person is Christian morality.

This living reality is proclaimed in many ways at many different levels. The different levels and different ways in which it is proclaimed are the various levels of proclamation and promulgation that we call law.

The first level of law is the common experience of urgency to be and become somebody according to the image presented by the real experience of being one's self in the human situation. The vision and experience of urgency in this first experience is commonly spoken of as the "natural law." It is unwritten; it is the common experience of the urgency of being human. It is the moral experience out of which there arises a moral conscience and consciousness in the individual and in the group. Out of this consciousness, proclamations and affirmations are spelled out about the expectations and responsibilities belonging to the group and its members that become the various levels of what is called positive law. Positive in reference to law does not mean "not negative," but rather, refers to the manner and source of promulgation. It means that the law is "posited" or put into writing in order to achieve a more effective promulgation in the community.

Legislation is the process of framing and promulgating the positive law. The legislative process established in any given society reflects the moral attitudes and premises of the culture. Primary moral attitudes of the culture are its judgments about right and wrong. A significant moral premise of any culture is the judgment and practice about the function of positive law in achieving the moral ideal.

Jesus proclaimed his gospel in a specific cultural environment of conflicting moral attitudes. It was not simply a conflict between the biblical faith of the religion of the Jews as against the Roman paganism, but the conflict and issue addressed by Jesus when he said "Render to Caesar the things that are Caesar's and to God the things that are God's." (Mt. 22/21)

The Jews themselves were at a point of crisis of survival in their own history. The crisis was essentially a moral crisis about the meaning and the function of law.

Observing the prescriptions of the positive ritual law was not the keeping of the Laws of the Covenant. When the temple was destroyed by Titus, there was no failure in the observance of the ritual law. It was even a high point of excellence in the observance of the ritual prescriptions. The failure of the Jews was a moral failure. It was the failure to become the people they were called to be by accepting the moral responsibilities of the gospel preached to them. The promise of their own covenant was a promise for them to keep and make come true by fulfilling the moral responsibility of making the promise come true for all other people. They failed their own covenant by claiming exclusive privilege for themselves and refusing to admit others to their covenant with God. They refused their call to be the people of God and to be a people for all others. It was a moral failure of covenant law even while the positive laws were being fulfilled to the letter.

In the history of the Church, the Reformation experience was a crisis of authority. It appeared on the surface as a question of the competence of the teaching and governing authority of the Church, but at its root was the issue of the moral dimension of faith in the Scriptures and the authority of the Church over the conscience of its members. It became a question of the competence of canonical authority in matters of conscience, and morality became primarily a doctrinal issue. A prime example today is the confusion and the disagreement between the teaching-law of the church and the conscience of the faithful in matters of birth control.

The consciences of many are trapped in an oppressive legalism which precludes and denies freedom of conscience. In the matter of moral decision about keeping the law, one must ask which is the authentic question: "What does the law permit?" or What does the law forbid?" Legalism requires that a person ask, "What does the law permit?" Legalism leaves the person free to choose only what the law permits and forbids the person to do anything not permitted by the law. Presuming the authenticity of the positive law, a prohibitive law is not a violation of freedom and it is reasonable to be required to ask, "What does the law forbid?" Prohibitive laws can place reasonable limitations on our freedom.

Clericalism in the Church is a form of legalism. Clerical privilege and immunity is a legalistic establishment and lay people are forbidden to do many things that are within their right and sacramental competence simply because they are not permitted by law. In fact, much of what is called liturgical renewal is still put in legalistic terms when it is spoken of in terms of liturgical functions that the lay people are now permitted to exercise. A lay person does not proclaim the gospel by permission of the hierarchy, but by his right as a believer.

To be required to ask "What does the law forbid?" is a reasonable search into the limit of freedom and any apparent conflict of rights. When there appears to be a conflict, the law itself resolves the issue because the lesser right ceases to exist in the presence of the higher right. In apparent conflict of rights, persons with the lesser rights really do not give up their rights. Their rights cease to exist in the presence of the higher right. The starving man has a right to a loaf of bread and has the moral power to exercise his right by taking it and eating it.

Our moral sense is severely lacking in appreciation of the rights of the corporate person. We have mentioned before that in our culture, the corporate person is mostly only an abstraction or a legal contrivance. Laboring people have had to organize and meet legal requirements in order to be considered a legal person with rights recognized and protected by law. The civil law can only define and measure. Civil law has defined and measured the rights of the individual and legally corporate persons. Civil law is severely limited in its competence to meet the needs and the rights of legally unincorporated poor and the oppressed. In the confrontation of the "haves" and the "have nots," the "haves" have their rights to be well defined by the law and the "have nots" must bear a burden of proof for the very existence of their rights. The "preferential option for the poor" has no legal status. Every person, individual or corporate, has the right to be fully person. Freedom is the power to have what is needed. Freedom puts the law to work, because freedom itself is the first law.

14
ANGELS
Nothing Better Than Being Human

OUR TRADITIONAL CULTURAL AND THEOLOGICAL IMAGE of man has been so poor that we distorted the image of the cosmic structure to accommodate humanity in its lowly status. We have compared man to God and have emphasized the inequality and difference and lost the awareness of the greatness of the image and likeness. We have used our philosophy to provide criteria for our judgment and conclusion about God. This whole process has not only reduced our image of God, but the image of man has suffered by the comparison.

In the process, being human has lost its place at the head of the cosmic process. Image and likeness has been reduced to the ontological category of analogy and we have become "something like God," but vastly different, with the cultural and theological emphasis on the difference. We lost our place at the head of the universe and were separated from God by an infinite gap or chasm which has left us disconnected from God in the organic structure of the universe and further disconnected and alienated by sin.

The most devastating consequence of the faulty human and cosmic image is a faulty vision of God and a gratuitous assumption of the adequacy of the categories in which we speak of God. Infinity attributed to God created a chasm between the infinite creator and finite creature which, somehow, has to be reduced if not closed. In this view, man is so finite and, at best, so far from God and the universe so incomplete and unfinished with the creation of man, that God simply would have to do better to have a universe worthy of him. The assumed infinite gap simply could not be tolerated.

Infinite gap denies, destroys and forbids a sense and an awareness of the nurturing comforting saving nearness of the presence that God is. Our cultural image of God and the universe has created the gap and the angelic order becomes the contrivance to close it. We have no need of angels if we really believe in God. We not only live in the immediate presence of God, but we are being breathed by God in the ongoing process and presence; we could not be closer than that. We are constantly totally dependent. God speaks us and speaks to us. We are involved in an immediate interpresence with God. The ancients for whom God was distant used the mythology of angels to speak of involvement with God in his universe. Our involvement with God involves the confrontation between good an evil.

In our tradition of faith, in our culture and in our Scripture, we have spoken mythologically about the struggle between good and evil. Creation itself is presented as a confrontation between good and evil, in which God does not create the world out of nothing but out of chaos by overcoming it. In the creative process, Adam and Eve are tested by the devil, a personification of the presence of evil. This same devil is the personification of evil and envy of the people that Jesus must confront in the temptations as presented in the synoptic gospels before he enters upon his mission.

Mythology is an affirmation of faith. Our mythology about angels, good and bad, was in its origin an affirmation about our real involvement in the struggle between good and evil. Good and evil are real and will always be with us. Mythology about angels has been an effective way to affirm our involvement in the struggle and to promise victory.

Mythology is an affirmation of faith about a real world. It is important for us to not forget or deny reality when we personally or culturally outgrow the myths that affirm reality.

Angels and devils are a mythology about our own personal involvement with good and evil and an affirmation of the personal nature of good and evil. Santa Claus is a myth, but Christmas giving continues when people no longer believe in Santa Claus. Outgrowing the myths about angels and devils should bring us to a deeper awareness and personal concern about the reality of good and evil and about moral responsibility. We must not outgrow the mythology by allowing good and evil to become mere abstractions or by losing our sense of urgency in moral decisions.

We have borrowed angels from an ancient Persian cosmology. The Book of Job borrows Satan from this cosmology. Satan is not evil but a kind of district attorney in the court of the gods holding people responsible for their actions. There are levels of functions and status in the court as reflected in the "nine choirs of angels" whose names and functions we have borrowed for our theology about the existence, structure and purpose of the angelic order. Cherubim, Seraphim, etc., are their real Persian names which we have adopted for our own theology. There were intrigue, conspiracy and treachery in the court. It came to a showdown and, of course, the good angels won and bad angels lost and went to hell, a place "prepared for the devil and his angels." (Matthew. 25:41) This has, also, provided our theology with a system for reward and punishment.

We must remember a cosmology is not a theology. Every person is somehow a believer. The first premise is a premise of faith. The cosmological first premise is mostly cultural. Image of person and his/her universe are really one premise. The Persian cultural cosmology of God *up there* somehow dealing with us *down here* permeated other cultures of the time including the Semitic. No doubt, there were many elements of this Persian cosmology in the culture of the people of Palestine at the time of Christ, including the world image of Jesus himself. It would have been part of their geocentric flat-earth image of themselves in their universe.

We develop this point to make a point. Our faith and theology, formal and informal, are always in context. When a believer says my God made the world, it is his God and his world he is speaking about. His God is God to him and his world is world to him, God as he knows him and world as he knows it. He may think the world is flat, but whatever it is, his God made it. His geology is poor, but his faith is good. He may think his God lives in a big house on the mountain top. His theology, geology and cosmology are poor, but his faith is good. In this matter, there is a comedy and a tragedy of errors.

For example, in the Galileo incident, we made a matter of astronomy a teaching of the Church and made the Bible a teacher of astronomy to our eternal embarrassment. The Church and the Bible teach God's man and man's God. This teaching must be in a contextual awareness and the sun and the earth and the stars, etc., enter the text. They can be nothing else but the sun and earth and stars of the speaker. Therefore, in the process, the circling sun or the flat earth are only contextual, and by all the demands and rights of Scripture and of all literature, they are neither affirmation or denial of anything, especially not of anything about God's people and people's God.

We have used the context as affirmation or denial in many instances with the claim that Scripture says this or that. Probably, the Book of Genesis suffers most here and the book is blamed for making many and poor contextual inferences about anthropology, biology, astronomy, physics, etc. The gospels and all the rest of Scripture suffer the same abuse. Genesis proclaims that Adam came from God as origin and is totally dependent upon Him. Genesis affirms nothing about the sciences, but in context, it shows the world view held by the writer. It affirms or denies nothing about the manner or the process of creation, how it happened, when or where it happened in our chronology or history. To quote Genesis for or against a theory of evolution is unscientific and is a violation of all rules of literary interpretation and a faithless abuse and perversion of the text of the word of God.

Our theology has made gratuitous assumptions from the cosmological context of the Scripture. It has compounded the errors by using the Scripture as proof text for our cultural images. We have reduced and denied the scriptural affirmation of "spirit" and "image of God" by putting "spirit" into the Greek universal category of non-matter, and image into the category of analogy—something "like," but vastly "different." Very simply, a pagan Greek cultural image of man which antedated the Christ by centuries in its origin, which happened to be the prevailing cultural image at the time of Christ, prevailed when the gospel was preached in that culture. The gospel did not Christianize or baptize the Greek image. The Greek image dominated and paganized the scriptural image in the name of the gospel. People in our culture will say, *"We are only human,"* and even with the resurrection of Jesus they will hold on to the angels to fill the gap between us and God.

It is not a question of existence of angels. The Scripture out of the Old Testament into the gospels makes direct and positive affirmations about angels, and the word "angel" remains the root of the word used for the proclamation of the "GOOD NEWS"—*evangelizing*—and all of its derivatives.

The question is not "Are there angels?" but rather, "What are angels?" The Hebrew word is *"Malach Yahweh"*—*"Angel of God."* It is a beautiful and direct way to express the reality of the presence of God that we have spoken about in symbol. All creatures are the real symbolic presence of God. When this creature is specifically the bearer of Good News, it becomes *"Malach Yahweh"*—*angel of God*, speaker for God. Prophets are "angels." The name for "Gabriel," our favorite angel, is not very "angelic" in its etymology. The name proclaims that this messenger is *"Gaber El"*—God's "he-man," "God's hero." The name is more of an affirmation of a human than a so-called angelic presence.

Much more could and should be said about this strange cosmology, but we must return to the purpose of introducing the matter in the first place. The introduction of angels as an order of being higher than man has reduced man in the image of God. Man and woman are the real image and the introduction of an angelic order has reduced the glory and dignity of being truly human. The prime example is its implication for Mary and Jesus. The cosmic and human image in the culture has prevailed as premise for "Mariology" and "Christology." It is so inadequate even for God's purposes to be *only human* that we have had to make Mary a unique exception. In this compulsion, we have contrived a theology of "Immaculate Conception" and of "assumption" to provide the exception to the rule, and keep her truly human.

Mary is not the exception! She is the rule and is presented in Scripture as "the authentic human believer, the totally faithful bride of Yahweh." In her faith, the Old Testament is a complete success. In Mary, every promise is fulfilled. All that God has in mind for his people is achieved in this woman by her being *totally authentically human*.

If in the premises, it is not good enough for Mary to be *only human*, it is much worse for her son. His works could not be explained in the categories of the system if he is only human. A "hypostatic union" of natures—divine and human—is then contrived to provide adequate cause for his works. His humanness becomes a "shadow" humanity which does not even allow him to be a human person, but somehow the bearer of a divine presence that is really doing all the work behind the scenes.

He is "Word made flesh." By being totally authentically human, he is the total speaking presence of God. His resurrection is his *human achievement*—the ultimate revelation of all that it means to be human—to be image of God. Everything that God has to say about himself, he says here. We must not let our culture forbid us to "learn of him" for the man that he is—the true image of God.

This "Word made flesh" is not the revelation of an exception to the rule of being human, but again he is the Rule, the Way, the Truth and the Life. In him, it is revealed that there is nothing better than being human. All affirmations about angels, notwithstanding, human person is not only the best creature God has created, but the best creature God could create and still be a creature. He proclaims his image in his spirit, the human spirit. He gives us the spirit that is God. It is not less than God because it is given or because it is human. It is human because it is being received and we are totally dependent. The more we receive, the more dependent we are, and the more dependent, the more human.

Let me present an illustration of how we have systematically denied the image and have even forged the scriptural documentation to make it fit our cultural image and doctrine. In the middle thirties, the Confraternity Edition of the psalms and the New Testament was prepared and published. Given all the circumstances, this was a very credible effort to bring the faithful reader an English rendering that was faithful to all the documents that came closest to the original sources. The translators were working on Psalm 8, which is an acclamation of the power and glory of the name of God as proclaimed in creation. In speaking of the glory of man in verse 5, the psalm affirms "you have made him *little less than Elohim*," which would mean "*little less than god*," as the translators wanted to render it. The bishops in charge of the project had a theological scruple about man being "little less than god" as being too good for man and directed that the text be rendered "little less than angels." This was published and remained in the Confraternity edition of the psalms. In the contemporary versions, the text reads, "little less than a god."

The first point to be noted in this incident is that "little less than god" was not only considered to be too good to be said about man and that if it was said at all, it would have to be said about angels who are presumed to really exist and to be better than man and closer to God. It was all done on the theological assumption of the existence of an order of personal beings called angels, and the creation, existence and function of angels are assumed in theology and in practice as a teaching of the Church.

Our traditional patterns and practices of prayer likewise presume the existence of an angelic order of intercessors and caretakers. It is held that there are angels above and beyond number, each one with a personal identity. The existence of personal guardian angels is likewise commonly held as a teaching of the Church. Angels have been structured into our world in an attempt to make it a better world with a better God. Is the world better with or without angels? If the world needs angels, it could be only because the world would be incomplete and unfinished without them. Psalm 8 affirms that man is the crowning glory of all creation. The gospel affirms that the resurrection of Jesus is the ultimate human achievement and the ultimate work of God's creative power. Evil which is sin and death are being confronted and overcome. Creation is at its final stage in the resurrection of Jesus. Our human freedom in the person of the Risen One is God's most glorious creation. Jesus being raised up in the glory in us is the ultimate glory of God.

Creation is in its final stage in the resurrection, but it is not yet complete. Everything yet to be done is within the resurrection, and the creative power by which it will be done is the resurrection power. The creative act and movement is the giving of the spirit which is holy. Holiness is humanness and humanness is holiness which we hold in common with God by which we are his image. God possesses his holiness in giving it to us. We and all of creation are in the process of receiving the spirit that is God by our own giving of the spirit. God is totally God to the world in giving his spirit and we are totally created image of God in receiving his spirit and possessing the spirit that is God in giving the spirit to others. To be human is to be good enough for God.

15
CHRISTOLOGY

"WHO DO YOU SAY THAT I AM"

TO BEGIN OUR DISCUSSION OF CHRIST, let us first consider Mary, the wife of the man Joseph, and the mother of the man Jesus. Historically, we have in this matter a classic case of a poor theology and a beautiful faith. Authentic faith will always prevail over poor theology and we can thank God for that. Mary deserves the place of honor that she has in the hearts of the Christian faithful even if theologians really haven't given good explanation or reasons for it.

It all started very innocently with the title "son of God." This title did not make its first appearance in Luke 1/35. "And so the child will be Holy and called the son of God." Luke borrows the title from the Book of Daniel 7/14. The Book of Daniel was a very popular book in those troubled times, from which book he also borrows for this story a key character by the name of Gabriel, who in each instance explains the meaning and promise of the word of God to a troubled believer. "Son of God" is the ultimate title for humanity, and affirmation of full and authentic humanity achieved by believing in the Word of God: it is in no way an affirmation of categorical substantial divinity.

"Son of God" means something quite different to the Semite believer than it does to the Greek philosopher. For the Greek, "son" means an affirmation of origin by generation in a communication of nature to another person, as we have "begotten not made," etc., in our creed. For the Semite believer, the title "son of God" means the affirmation of origin by faith in the creative process of interpresence. This is the point at which we have entered the world of the Greek culture and have begun a theological process making doctrine and dogma about Jesus the object of faith, which culminates in the doctrinal decrees of the Council of Ephesus. The Greek philosopher forgot his own rules for logical distinction, and "generation" becomes "origin" itself, not just the means by which "origin" is taken. In the same categorical logic, "son of God" had to be of the *same divine nature* as God who generated him. Hence, by logical conclusion from unwarranted premises we have contrived the "divinity of Christ," the keystone for the whole structure of dogmatic teaching of the Church about Jesus.

If Jesus is the "son of God" by generation in nature, and Mary is the mother of the son, logic demands that she who is the mother of a son who is God, is "Mother of God," *Theotokos*. We made Jesus *substantially* God and from there had to contrive the term, *Theotokos*, Mother of God, for Mary his mother.

This logic prevailed at the Council of Ephesus in 425 A.D. and the people celebrated in the streets in candlelight and torch processions because their most favored believer and Holy One had been given the ultimate honor. The honor and favor of their faith was authentic, because honor and favor are due Mary for her own faith. Both the faith and the theology have perdured till our own time, but now the faith that honors Mary has achieved a new level of security and possession, while the theology of Ephesus is fading. The question "What is most proper, most honoring title for Mary" has been answered in the process of the Second Vatican Council. People still fear and ask "What has happened to Mary?" and contemporary theologians are accused of ignoring and even belittling her. Nothing is farther from the truth. Mary never had it so good.

In the first place, Vatican II has not proclaimed a new doctrine about her, nor has it accorded her a new title as was quite generally expected. Vatican II has given Mary her due by affirming that we do not go to the Church to learn about Mary, but that we go to Mary to learn about the Church. As this Woman in her moment of faith is the whole people of God, she is the temple of, the temple "that is" the presence of God. She is the *pre-church*, the Daughter of the Most High, and of *her faith* is born the Holy One, the son of the Most High who is the Christ. In her, Yahweh-God has found a totally faithful bride of whom the Christ-Church is being born.

In regard to titles, many of the faithful and many of the Council Fathers entered the Second Vatican Council with the expectation of another Ephesus, that the crowning glory and achievement of the Council would be the official proclamation of another and a final title to the long list in the Litany of Loretto, "Mary, Mediatrix of All Grace," and the streets of Rome would be filled with joyous celebration.

What happened at Vatican II is something much more consistent with the character of the honoree, a very restrained and mostly implicit affirmation that *"One title alone is necessary."* She is the *Believer in the Word of God.* There is no more to say. There is nothing better to say. This title says it all. Luke puts it into perspective, when he says in 8/19, "rather blessed is she who hears the Word of God and keeps it." In fact, Luke, our best loved proclaimer of Mary and the glory of Mary's faith, was himself satisfied with the same title, only he had a different word for it. His word was "virgin."

Luke's Annunciation story is set in a temple scene and all the characters are temple characters and the temple itself is the presence of (that is) God. "Virgin" is a title, a name for temple servant, a name which means "faithful one" or "faithful servant" in the presence of God. In this instance, the name "virgin" in the text or in the minds of the original readers had no reference at all to actual sexual experience or its absence. It was an affirmation of fidelity and faithful service. It meant "believer in the Word of God." Whatever the value or the credit may be for not having had sexual relations with a man, it pales into insignificance in comparison to the credit that is given for being a true believer in the Word of God and his promises. Elizabeth proclaims, "Blessed is she who believed that the promise made to her by the Lord would be fulfilled." Luke 1/45.

The use of the word and title "virgin" in this proclamation of conception and birth is neither affirmation nor denial of anything about the physiology and sexual experience or lack of it, for the principals. It is a simple, plain and beautiful affirmation that the child is a child of faith, that he is born of the faith of his parents, that faith is his origin, and that the sexual experience or lack of it in his human origin doesn't even enter into the account or into consideration. What reason would there be even to consider it a factor or to think it would make a difference, or above all, what good reason would there be for making the manner of his conception and birth an exception from that of all the others with whom he is one, and "like us in all things?"

As we have mentioned for Luke's original readers, "virgin" was a title of honor and credit for faithfulness, "believer in the Word of God" and "Son of God" itself was a title of faith. The infancy narrative of Luke is an extension of the origin story of Genesis. Genesis affirms in the Patriarch stories that the real origin of the people of God is not told in a biological genealogy but that their real and true origin is faith, that they are a people born of faith.

What is true of the "Old" people is true of the "New," and the new people are being born of the same but new faith in the same God, who shows new signs and new wonders in a new creation. There is real "fathering" and real "mothering." But when a later culture than that of the writing began to set the meaning of the words of scripture and insisted the scripture be interpreted in its own cultural categories, then "son of God" became "an affirmation of origin by generation in a communication of nature to another person." "Son of God" in the New Testament as title of honor for faith in God as applied to the man Jesus was made to take on a meaning entirely different from the intention of the original writer.

Out of the Old Testament, "Son" or "Daughter" of God would have to be within the process set at the beginning, where in the creation story itself, God's "creative wording" is "fathering."

This process did not fail. There is no need to introduce any emergency tactic or a rescue operation from *out there*. The Father's established creative presence is adequate. Salvation is not a rescue mission in which we are snatched from the teeth of the Dragon or from the fiery pit. We do more honor to God and to man; we make God a better creator, and man a better creature, if we let the whole work of Christ from start to finish, from his birth to his Resurrection, come within the dimension of being fully and authentically human. The Christ, the New Adam, did what the Old Adam failed to do. And New Adam did it in spite of failure; the Father's plan works in spite of the failure of man. We must let Mary and Jesus come entirely within the ordinary plan, and not require that they be exceptions. To keep it human does more honor to God, more honor to Mary and her son and more honor to us. The work of Redemption, from promise to fulfillment, from birth to resurrection, is a human achievement, an achievement of the people we all are; it is not just a work done for us by special divine intervention, by exception or superhuman persons. The work was all within the "ordinary" human process and is still going on in what we are pleased to call the *Church*.

Our cultural image, however, of what it means to be human is so poor that to be *only human* seems to be not enough. In this image, human sexuality is part of the embarrassment of being *only human*, a constant reminder that we are *only human*, and a constant impediment to rising above being *only human*.

From the moment that the Greek cultural image of man prevailed in Christian theology, there was the compulsion to remove anything and everything sexual from the human origin of Jesus, because of the conviction that anything sexual in his human origin would have defiled him. The only way that could be done is to have him born of a "virgin undefiled" and the title "virgin" takes on an entirely different meaning in our theology than it ever had in Scripture. From our theology it has worked its way into our culture and we have a new and different criterion for judging human behavior. To become somehow sexless or unsexed has become a mark of excellence or even superiority in the achievement of Christian holiness.

In the process, human sexuality has become something to be tolerated, a strange and mysterious contrivance for the procreation of the race, creative for the race, but potentially destructive and constantly threatening for the individual. Marriage became a situation that *permitted* sexual relationship, and non-marriage, with a promise of no sexual experience, became a *higher way of life*. Chastity became bi-level, chastity by vow was honorable and heroic, chastity by law became the minimum requirement for avoiding hell. Chastity by vow was accepted as being honorable and heroic and it came to be imposed upon clerics as a discipline of the Church. It was considered to be, and was accepted as a reasonable expectation, that those called to a *higher life* and called to a status of privilege and immunity in the Church should measure up to the popular and cultural image of hero and saint, and the vow of chastity or promise of a life of celibacy was required before Holy Orders. At the time the discipline was first imposed, and for centuries later, the image of celibate commitment and heroic self-denial was an image of honor, faithful commitment to ministry and service in Christian society.

We must remember in the present reassessment of the issue, first of all, that celibacy of the clerics in the Church is only a discipline; it is not a divine institution. Secondly, we must be aware that the cultural attitude has changed. The so-called "sexual revolution" is not all bad. People are becoming comfortable with sex, and are becoming aware of the function and role of sex in achieving the integrity of personality and personal identity. Many have become comfortable in assuming responsibility for sexual behavior and, of course, many have not, and very few have come to an awareness of the symbolic dimension of sex without which there cannot be a credible sexual morality.

Given the process and the problem, the cultural image has changed and is changing for the better, and in the cultural image the celibate is no longer a hero or saint, but a rather wierd exception committed to a strange behavior. Witness to faith demands a credibility and celibacy is certainly no longer instant credibility. Celibacy by choice in favor of ministry and in favor of a real marriage commitment of service to the real corporate person who is Christ is certainly valid within the Christian community. True as this may be, celibacy by discipline is no longer prophetic witness to the culture, or an invitation to the Gospel way of life or an assurance and promise of genuine ministry. When celibacy as a discipline has itself become the issue, when even the Catholic faithful would largely prefer that it no longer be required as a discipline, and would largely prefer to have a married clergy, it is hard to find a good reason to retain celibacy as a discipline of the Church.

These problems and issues are discussed in this chapter about Mary because they are a part of the confused context in which we believe in the Scripture and in which we believe in the first believer who is Mary. Mary, in many ways, has been victim of our cultural premises and prejudice. There is no need to rescue her by making her an exception to the rule or to the image. It is in Mary that we can begin to rescue and restore the image of being human. We must cease to defend her from being *only human* by making her *superhuman*. We must see her for what she is and come to the vision of the glory of what it is to be truly and fully human.

In Mary, there is the return of the Spirit to man and the beginning of the return of man to God. Mary remains the point of our entry and re-entry into the creative process which now, because of sin, must also be redemptive. In the process, we must regain and redeem humanity that was lost before we can achieve the glory of being human that is promised in the faith of Mary and is achieved in the resurrection of the son that is born of her faith. The faith of Mary is our entry into the process.

In the authentic human process, the Christ must not only be authentically "mothered" in faith, but he must also be really and authentically "fathered" by a *real* father. By a strange logic from strange premises about the "divinity" of the Christ we have presumed that he didn't need a real human father or that the presence of a real human father would threaten or contradict his true character. The man, Jesus, has a *real* father and his name is Joseph.

Joseph also has suffered from our fears and theological scruples and denials. He has been called "adoptive" father, "foster" father, even "putative" father, because everyone is afraid of the implications of calling him the *real* father, as the Gospel does. Matthew and Luke speak of the father and mother of Jesus without disclaimers or limiting qualifications that somehow say "father, but not really." His name is Joseph for good reason. He is new Joseph fathering a new people, rising by faith out of the bottom of the pit. Mary believed in the promises of God when it seemed all was lost and Joseph believed in Mary when it seemed that she and her unborn child should be cast out in disgrace.

Here there is no affirmation and denial of the physiological or biological origin of the child, but there is affirmation that there is no fathering more real than fathering by faith. Why should it not be true of Jesus when it is true for all of us, that there is for any child no fathering or mothering that is more real than believing and being believed in. The gospel story, like the whole Bible is a story about believers. Faith is the common denominator, every character of the gospel is a unique believer and Joseph is no exception.

Luke and Matthew, in the infancy narratives, do not paint a "Christmas card," or an idyllic pastoral domestic scene. Their background is not soft color, soft light and soft music. Their background is the Book of Daniel. It is impending doom, crisis, extremity, survival against all odds. It is the apocalyptic urgency of the bottom of the pit. There is no place to go but up. There has to be a future, even if it seems that all is lost. But "all this took place to fulfill what the Lord had spoken through the prophet: Look! The virgin is with child and gives birth to a son whom they will call Emmanuel, a name which means God-is-with-us. When Joseph woke up he did what the Angel of the Lord told him to do; He took his wife to his home...she gave birth to a son and Joseph named him Jesus." (Matthew 1/24-25) The ultimate privilege and right of the real father is to name the child and there could be no better or more positive scriptural affirmation of the real fatherhood of Joseph than the simple statement "and Joseph named him Jesus."

We have spoken here of Mary and Joseph not only out of a scriptural and cultural perspective but in the full context of our contemporary faith. We do our believing in a real existential cultural environment and communicate our faith in the language and images of the culture of the moment. Contemporary culture has moved from abstract and romantic images and ideas to real live "role models" in presenting the image of the persons we ought to be. Role models are more attractive and more convincing than abstract or romantic images but Scripture and revelation present more than role models, revelation presents the living presence of the true believer. That living presence is not somebody that I should be like or that I should imitate, but always someone I should be.

The real Christ still needs real fathering and real mothering and true believers are real Joseph and real Mary, nurturing the real living Christ. The Gospel does not present Jesus as the role model that we should imitate or copy. We should not ask "What would Mary or Joseph or Jesus do if they were here?"

Rather we should move forward with the confidence and courage of true faith, by being the true believers of our own time and place. It is not that we have replicated the faith of Mary and Joseph in our time but that the faith of Mary and Joseph has become even better in us, is constantly becoming the faith of the Risen One, and by this faith we do not enter with him into Glory, but we are him. The resurrection glory of this moment is the achievement of the faith of all those who believe themselves into him into God.

"And who do you say that I am?" "Thou art the Christ, the Son of the Living God." (Matthew 16/16.)

"Who do you say that I am?" remains a burning question and has become even a divisive issue since it was first asked at Caesaraea Philippi. Peter's answer at that time was a simple uncomplicated statement and affirmation of faith that was accepted and honored by the Christ himself. Peter said simply, "Thou are the Christ, the Son of the Living God." And Jesus said, "Simon, Son of Jonah, you are a blessed man, because it was no human agency that revealed this to you but my father in heaven." (Matthew 16/18.) The question could not have been asked more authentically, nor could the answer have been validated and approved more authoritatively. The question remains the same and, in spite of the validity and adequacy of the answer, there is confusion and controversy about who he is within the body of those who profess to believe in him. His title is "the Christ" and his name is "Jesus."

The name and title "Christian" is given to those who profess to believe in him. The critical and determining belief about the Christ is considered to be faith in his divinity and, very simply by this criterion, a Christian is one who believes that Jesus, the Christ, is God. This all seems simple enough—a simple answer to a simple question. There is, however, question about the question itself and question about the answer. "Who do you say that I am?" remains the valid question. It remains a valid question when asked by the Christ and evokes a personal response and affirmation of the believer—a conversation in the first and second person. It really becomes a different question when it is asked by theologians in the third person. Theology about the Christ is quite different than faith in the Christ and theological conclusions are far removed from the urgency and immediacy of the revealing presence. The living, speaking and spoken word is the proper object of faith, not the theological conclusion.

It is not my purpose here to restate a theology about the Christ, but to arrive at an affirmation about who he really was and is. For the late nineteenth and twentieth century, the question about the Christ was a question about the historical "Christ" and the "Christ" of faith. In our times, the question about the Christ is an issue between fundamentalists and liberals, but remains a question about his divinity. There is a general belief that to be the Christ of promise and fulfillment of Sacred Scripture, the real Christ would have to be more than human, and to be more than human, he would have to be God. The culture provides the context and furnishes many of the premises for the reasoning of believers. The cultural premise about being human was a human race deeply flawed by sin. Being created in the image of God was victim of a false philosophical premise that reduced image itself to a distant similarity in which image became something like but vastly different. Such a race is unworthy and incompetent without any power to set things right with God. For such believers, the Savior of such a human race would have to be more than the race itself could provide, and on that premise the image of the Savior Christ was built as divine, in good faith, but poor theology.

In this cultural, historical and theological process, fundamentalists have been and remain the champions of orthodoxy with a seige mentality and with a fear that so-called liberals threaten to destroy the word and the work of God by even opening the question about the identity of the Christ. The Gospel question "Who do you say that I am?" is still spoken directly to every believer and must be answered by the believer in the context of the revelation in which it is being asked. In the context of contemporary revelation, there is a sense of sacrament and presence which goes much deeper into living reality than the traditional categories which were the context of the old Christology. When we explain image in the terms of sacrament, we affirm that a person, by being human, is a real speaking presence of God—that human person is sacrament of God. To say that Jesus is Sacrament of God is to say that Jesus, by being totally authentically human is the real presence of God. The God-thing for God to do is to be a fathering "worder"—this is simply God being God. The one produced in the fathering wording is Son word, "Word made flesh," the real living speaking presence of the Fathering God. This is real presence of real divinity. It is real living divinity made present by the affirmation and authentication of humanity, not by reduction to the category of instrumental cause.

This is not the introduction of a new dimension, a new reality or a new system at the historical moment of the person we know as the Christ, but a recovery and a return to the original plan of creation. Human freedom had failed. It was not part of the plan that freedom should fail, but the plan was so good that it could handle the failure by overcoming it. It was achieved by one person, Jesus the Christ, becoming totally authentically human. Sacramentality is a human achievement. One Christ person is person before God for all other persons, born for all, speaks for all, lives for all, dies for all and arises from the dead for all. He does this, not as agent for all, but in the one Spirit that is God, he really and truly is all others doing all these human things. (In the last sentence the verb "is" has to be a transitive verb.) There is a beautiful mutuality in sacramentality. Christ is us and we are Christ; sacramentality is the achieved mutuality, it is the holy human Spirit at work.

Christology has to be put into the total creative process of human being and being human. There was the Christ Event in human history. Human history is an ongoing event in the Creative Presence of God. Everything that Jesus is or will be in the total human event is human. He did the human thing totally and perfectly and everything he was in doing it was human. We do not reduce or remove God by making the plan work. We bring this to a living, present urgency in our awareness that we are the Christ, and the Christ is us. This is totally authentic Christology.

16
THE QUESTION OF GOD

AN ANSWER BEFORE THE QUESTION

WE ARE INESCAPABLY ALWAYS INVOLVED in the question of God. Every age and every culture is characterized by how the God question is asked or not asked, how it is answered or not answered, or how it is recognized or ignored. The question is asked in different ways with different motives by many. Some think they have the answer, others deny that there is an answer and there are those who will say it is not even a question.

We will presume that it is a question. We will presume that we are believers speaking to believers for whom the question of God is always urgent, always open, always being asked, and always being answered. Every answer opens a new question. Everything we come to know tells us how much there is yet to know. Every question is a promise, not only of an answer but an answer that will bring joy, peace, the satisfaction of possession and presence and a new question.

A necessary part of the search is to learn how to ask the right question, how to exclude the wrong question, how and where to look for the right answer and what is the source of our knowledge. In our search the first question is "How do we get to know God."

As believers, we will start with the premise of *REVELATION*—that God has revealed Himself by speaking and that God is a speaking God. In this search, there is that way in which every believer is the first believer because each believer must make a discovery and at the same time each believer receives the faith from another. The process of receiving the faith from other is called a faith tradition. A faith tradition is more a process of identity than a content or a subject matter. Jesus Himself is born to us of the faith of Abraham, the first believer in our tradition.

Good theology is a faith search. Good theology is search for the right question. Good theology will have the faith premises to move in the right direction, to know the right question and to exclude the wrong or invalid question. Theology will have to establish its starting point and its direction in choosing one of the following questions to the complete exclusion of the other: "Do we know who God is by knowing who we are?" or "Do we know who we are by knowing who God is?"

The first question is itself the answer. We know who God is by knowing who we are. The first assurance of our faith and the first premise of our theology is that our God is not a hidden God. In the earliest revelations, it becomes clear that the appeal of Yahweh is that He does not hide, taunt and harass people from His secret hiding place but that His hand and presence is to be seen in His work. This is the first credibility in contrast to the gods hidden behind the idols of human creation. Wonder of wonders, here is a God who speaks and the crowning point of the whole process is "Word made flesh." "Word made flesh" is a summary statement, a simple and profound proclamation of the whole process and of the message. It is promise and promise fulfilled; it is the high point and summary of all creation. God-revealing and God-creating are the same God doing the same thing.

We are here concerned with the revealing or speaking aspect of the process and our question is : "What, where, when and how does God speak?" "Word made flesh" is the whole answer. It is all-inclusive. It is everything that God says. It is the what, where, when and how of God speaking but, wonder of wonders, it is also who.

Let us take the simple proclamation word by word and start with the word, "WORD." There is much to be set straight at this point at which the Greek philosophy has entered and has taken over the whole process. The philosophical dialect has become the idol. The old idols were dumb but this idol has spoken gibberish and has won the allegiance of generation after generation of the peoples. The culture that has become the "church" — that has made and still makes doctrine and dogma — the object of faith.

"Word" is not "*logos*." It is not "idea" or expression for idea. It has nothing to do with "idea" or its expression. Idea is not person. Idea is only "about" person and is a product of person. It is a contradiction to say that the idea is the person who has the idea. The "word that is made flesh" is the Hebrew "*dabar*." "*Dabar*" is *person-present-speaking*. "Word made flesh" means first of all *person-present*. It is an affirmation of presence *by speaking*. "Word of God" means word that is God — not word that belongs to God — but the speaking presence that God is.

"*FLESH*" is a very direct and unequivocal affirmation of total, real, existential humanity which is person-present. This person's name is Jesus, a real human person who by being the human person that he is, is the speaking presence of God. Our purpose is not to engage in a debate about Christological doctrine but to transcend doctrine and return to faith. We must return to that faith that is the awareness that we are the "Flesh" that the "Word" has become and is "becoming." Our being human and our human being is the revealing presence of God.

For the Greek this is too good to be true. In fact, it will be condemned to hell as blasphemous pantheism; it is simply an affirmation of what it really means to be human, to be "Word made Flesh." We must remember that God is not limited to our categories. His Word is His work. Sacrament is not an exercise in instrumental causality. "Word made Flesh" is sacrament. Every and all believers are the speaking presence that is God.

THE QUESTION OF GOD · 237

As to the question: "Do we know who we are by knowing who God is?" or "Do we know who God is by knowing who we are?"—we know who God is by knowing who we are. Being human and human being are the revelation of God. "Word made Flesh" is very humanistic and the theological search into the meaning of "Word made Flesh" is humanistic because there is no other way to know who God is than to know who we are and because who we are is where God tells it all.

With the current wave of fundamentalism, culturally, politically, sociologically and theologically, all humanism is condemned or at least suspect. All humanism is implicitly condemned by the label "secular." For the fundamentalist, "secular humanism" is the sin of the age and the root of all evil. This premise or prejudice distorts the Bible by trying to protect the Bible from any taint of humanism.

The whole Bible is the human affirmation of the faith response to God and, as it develops, the more authentically human the response becomes, the more and better the Word is proclaimed. The Resurrection is the ultimate response to the Father—the ultimate human achievement and proclamation of faith. The Resurrection is the on-going affirmation of the Good News that all is right with God.

It is the affirmation not only that there is nothing wrong with being human but that to be authentically human is the best that we can be without being God. It is never wrong to be human. It is always a glory to be human. The only thing that is wrong is to contradict or deny our humanity by sin. Sin is against God because it contradicts and denies humanity which is the speaking presence of God.

The Bible is the Word of God because it is an authentic human affirmation. In the broadest and deepest corporate sense, the Bible is "autobiographical." The people of God are a faith-people, a faith-person who proclaims his identity and faith experience in the Bible. In the first place, it does not pretend or claim to be the complete story or the whole picture.

The writing itself is not a "writing about." The very writing is itself the faith experience of being the people of God.

The writing has to be human in order to be real and to be true; the writing itself will reveal the limitations, faults and failings of the "autobiographer." The "autobiographer" has to speak in and out of a total, real existential environment out of his own awareness, experience and response to the events of his own time out of the corporate memory, telling and interpreting events past but kept present by the memory and the telling.

The Bible is always a real living person-present speaking. The person speaking remains living and present in the same spirit and in the same creative process of "Word made Flesh" in which the Resurrection continues to be real and living. We are the only and real and living body of the Risen One. "Word" is the living speaking presence of the person; "made flesh" is permanent creative establishment of the "autobiographer" as the person-present speaking. The speaking will at all times and in every instance reflect the total human existential situation and environment in which and from which it is spoken. The speaking itself is always an event that doesn't happen in a vacuum and the circumstances and writer's awareness of himself and his universe will be reflected in the writing.

There is no writing style that is unique for the Bible. The Bible is unique but it does not have its own literary style. Its style is human and its literary style is the literary style of the "autobiographer" of the moment and of the event of the writing. This style and the writing itself are the context for the faith affirmation about "God's man and man's God." The "autobiographer" is always a believer, even when it is hard for him to believe and he is always a real living human person: a person of his own time, place, culture, people, language, experience, and view of himself and his universe. For example, the "autobiographer's" view of the universe was geo-centric; for him the sun went around a stationery flat earth each day. His geocentrism will be reflected in the context of his writing without touching or in anyway reducing the credibility of his faith affirmation. The context will reflect his ideas about his universe and how it works but these are context and cannot be interpreted as scientific or historical affirmation or denial.

The Book of Genesis is perhaps the most abused by these demands. The Book of Genesis is the Book of Origins. Genesis affirms that all people and their world come from God and are totally dependent, that all people have a common origin in God and that our real origin in and from God is origin by faith. It is as much of an abuse of Scripture to use the Book of Genesis as an argument against evolution as it is to use it for evolution. The book is an affirmation that we and our universe have our origin in God, that we are totally dependent, that we are responsible for "keeping" our universe and for nurturing the life we have received. It is interesting to note in this connection that the Patriarch stories of the Book of Genesis were written in the form in which we have them in the final century before the birth of Christ. The slaves who escaped from Egypt about 1250 B.C. really had no ethnic identity. They were not the biological descendants of Abraham who lived about 1850 B.C. but in the faith they received from Abraham through Moses, they are the promised progeny of Abraham. This faith, as in Mary and Joseph, is the origin of Jesus and in Him is our origin as the people of God. The Book of Genesis and the whole Bible is an affirmation of faith origin and birth, not a record for biological generation.

The unique character of the Bible as the Word of God is ordinarily attributed to or explained by a process called "inspiration." Whatever it is or however it comes about, the result is that the words of a believing man or woman become and are the Word of God. Much of the attempt to explain how this comes about — to explain inspiration — is *Deus ex machina.* Its value and quality are its truth not its freedom from error. The Word of God is not true because He said it; He said it because it is true. The "word" in the scriptural sense is "person-present-speaking not just the idea, its expression, context or meaning. "Inspiration"—or "inspiritedness"—is a beautiful word for the process but the process includes the speaker *and* the believer or hearer, not just the speaker. There must be in the process a sacramental integrity, the transcending integrity by which the word is not the word until it is spoken and listened to. The "Book"—Bible—is not a book until it is being read as bread is not bread until it is given and eaten, as a bell is not a bell until it is rung and a song is not a song until it is sung. The Word of God is not the Word until it is believed in. The only real presence of the real speaking God is people who believe in Him. It is mystery hidden until discovered and entered by faith. This is inspiration. All faith is a gift of God. It is the divine initiative: God is always first. In the human faith experience, this divine initiative is a believer-speaker, Word made flesh, inviting and promising another becoming-believer to enter the presence of mystery and the mystery of presence. All of this is in the human spirit which is the Spirit that is God as entered and possessed by human believers. Whatever, wherever and however this takes place in the process of the human spirit is inspiration; it is mystery discovered and entered. Any attempt to define, analyze or explain it denies and contradicts the mystery.